Building better credit unions

Building better credit unions

Peter Goth, Donal McKillop and Charles Ferguson

First published in Great Britain in February 2006 by

The Policy Press
Fourth Floor, Beacon House
Queen's Road
Bristol BS8 1QU
UK

Tel no   +44 (0)117 331 4054
Fax no   +44 (0)117 331 4093
E-mail   tpp-info@bristol.ac.uk
www.policypress.org.uk

© Queen's University Belfast 2006
Transferred to Digital Print 2008

Published for the Joseph Rowntree Foundation by The Policy Press

ISBN 978 1 86134 829 6

British Library Cataloguing in Publication Data
A catalogue record for this report is available from the British Library.

Library of Congress Cataloging-in-Publication Data
A catalog record for this report has been requested.

Peter Goth is a researcher and Donal McKillop is Professor of Financial Services, both at Queen's University Belfast. Charles Ferguson is Senior Policy Adviser with Volunteer Development Scotland.

The Joseph Rowntree Foundation has supported this project as part of its programme of research and innovative development projects, which it hopes will be of value to policy makers, practitioners and service users. The facts presented and views expressed in this report are, however, those of the authors and not necessarily those of the Foundation.

The statements and opinions contained within this publication are solely those of the authors and not of The University of Bristol or The Policy Press. The University of Bristol and The Policy Press disclaim responsibility for any injury to persons or property resulting from any material published in this publication.

The Policy Press works to counter discrimination on grounds of gender, race, disability, age and sexuality.

Cover design by Qube Design Associates, Bristol.
Printed in Great Britain by Marston Book Services, Oxford.

Contents

List of tables

Acknowledgements

The authors wish to express their gratitude to Paul McDonnell for his research support in the preparation of this study. They would also like to thank the managers, board members and other senior officials of individual credit unions who gave of their time to participate in the case study elements of this research. The authors are also indebted to the Joseph Rowntree Foundation for the generous financial support given to this project. Finally, we are extremely grateful to the members of the Advisory Committee established by the Joseph Rowntree Foundation to comment on the work undertaken in the drafting of this report.

Introduction

Credit unions are not-for-profit, cooperative financial institutions. Traditionally, they have been seen as serving the financial services needs of disadvantaged communities and individuals. As the movement has developed, particularly in countries such as the US, Canada and Australia, credit unions have increasingly appealed to the professional classes and competed with other retail financial institutions for this client base. In the US, 43% of the population belong to a credit union, compared to 22% in Canada and 26% in Australia.

In the UK, the credit union sector has experienced solid growth in recent years, with membership increasing from 232,137 with assets of £124 million in 1991, to 697,560 members and assets of £789 million in 2001, to 814,538 members and assets of approximately £900 million by 2004. (These figures were derived from data taken from Northern Ireland [NI] credit unions' annual return forms and from the Financial Services Authority [FSA] [2001b, 2004].) However, this level of membership represents a penetration of less than 1% of the population, which is disappointing, especially when compared to a penetration rate of over 45% in the Republic of Ireland (HM Treasury, 1999). The low overall penetration does, however, mask the varying levels of success achieved by the movement within different regions of the UK. In NI, the movement is strongest, with about 26% of the population belonging to a credit union. Sibbald et al (2002) argue that part of the success of the movement in NI is due to the promotion of credit unions by organisations that already have an enshrined voice within NI, most notably the Catholic Church and, more recently, the Orange Order. The leaders of the British credit union movement, initially at least, were drawn from the immigrant communities of Ireland and the West Indies. Large numbers of Irish immigrants settled in the central and west regions of Scotland and it is no coincidence that the British movement is strongest in Scotland, with 35% of credit union members located in these regions. The rest of Scotland accounts for approximately 9% of Great Britain (GB) membership (Donnelly and Kahn, 1999; Donnelly, 2002). In 2004, there were 779 credit unions in the UK, of which 434 were located in England, 32 in Wales, 131 in Scotland and 182 in NI (FSA, 2004).

Although there is not widespread acceptance of credit unions by the general public in GB, there is acknowledgement by government that as 'third sector' lenders they have an important role to play in the provision of affordable credit, and many credit unions operate in areas of high financial exclusion (HM Treasury, 2005). The government has endeavoured to develop a framework aimed at broadening the appeal of credit unions in GB. The roots to this support for credit unions started in 1998 when a Treasury taskforce was established in order to investigate ways of promoting expansion of the sector in GB. The published report suggested a number of changes, many of which were placed into operation through legislative revisions to the 1979 Credit Union Act. In addition, the financial regulation of credit unions in GB transferred from the Registry of Friendly Societies to the FSA in July 2002, with an objective 'to increase consumer confidence in credit unions, which should enable them to grow and meet their wider social and financial objectives' (Strachan, 2001, p 1). More recently, in *Promoting financial inclusion* (HM Treasury, 2004), it was announced that 'to support the valuable work of credit unions and to boost the coverage, capacity and sustainability of the sector' (p 44) a growth fund for third sector lenders would be established, there would be a mapping of third sector lenders, and the Financial Inclusion Taskforce would consider ways in which the skills of volunteers and staff within the third sector could be enhanced.

In Scotland, the Scottish Executive introduced, in September 2003, a Capacity Fund of £1.1 million aimed at helping credit unions build their capacity and work towards self-sufficiency. In January 2005, the Scottish Executive launched its Financial Inclusion Action Plan, which sets out its work to support credit unions and the role credit unions can play in supporting financial inclusion. More recently, a state aid scheme has been approved to enable credit unions to receive public funding on the basis of a Service of General Economic Interest (SGEI). Under the SGEI scheme, financial support can be provided by the Scottish Executive and other public funders to enable credit unions to develop and provide a specific suite of products which meet the needs of financially and socially marginalised consumers.

In Wales, the Welsh Assembly (Welsh Assembly Government, 2004) describes how it supports credit unions as part of a wider agenda to develop a social economy and regenerate disadvantaged communities. Between 2001 and 2004, the Assembly delivered the Welsh Credit Union Strategy in partnership with the Association of British Credit Unions (ABCUL) and the Wales Cooperative Centre. This was supported by over £4 million of Assembly and Structural Funds, and its primary goal was to create a self-sustaining credit union movement by attracting and retaining members, and developing volunteers. In addition, the Debt Redemption and Money Advice scheme was launched on 16 September 2003 in partnership with the Assembly, the Wales Cooperative Centre, the Coalfields Regeneration Trust (CRT), money advisers and credit unions in South Wales, where the CRT operates. It helps to combat indebtedness by allowing credit unions to 'buy out' the existing debts of individuals who agree to become members. Since September 2004, the Assembly has not provided any new public funding for credit unions because of EU law relating to the provision of State Aid. However, it is believed that a block exemption for SGEIs, under which aid for credit unions will qualify, is forthcoming.

Although the movement in NI is much more successful than elsewhere in the UK, there is currently consultation under way on proposals for the modernisation of NI policy on credit unions (DETI [NI], 2004). It is anticipated that this review will result in a widening of the statutory powers available to the Registrar for Credit Unions in NI; a mandatory requirement that credit unions participate in a savings protection scheme; alterations to current limits on the size and condition of loans and savings/shareholders' accounts; the facility to offer a range of additional services; a widening of the common bond; and a removal of the cap on membership.

From these initial comments, it should be clear that there is increasing acceptance of the view that credit unions have a potentially important role to play in the provision of affordable credit to all sections of society, including those facing financial exclusion. It should also be evident that throughout the UK strenuous efforts are being made through legislative amendments to broaden the appeal of credit unions. It is also the case that, at least to date, only a limited number of UK credit unions can be viewed as successful.

Accepting these points, the primary objective of this study is to identify the factors, both qualitative and quantitative, driving differences in the performance of UK credit unions. More specifically, financial data and case study material are used to identify operational aspects which have contributed to the relative success of individual credit unions.

Within this general framework of trying to isolate factors behind successful credit union development, it is also important to be mindful of any changing trends within the sector. Two in particular stand out. The first is the establishment of new 'fast growth' credit unions, a number of which are sponsored by their local authority and have, in a very short time span, achieved significant membership levels. The second trend is the steady stream of mergers which has led to a fall in the overall number of credit unions in the UK, particularly during the last two years, when credit union numbers fell considerably each year. For example, in 2004 there were 779 credit unions in the UK, compared to 847 in 2003 (FSA, 2004). The fall in numbers occurred mostly in England, with a drop in credit union numbers from 487 to 434. In Wales, the fall was from 44 to 32; in Scotland, the drop was marginal from 134 to 131 while, in NI, the numbers remained unchanged at 182. These two trends will be considered from the perspective of whether they are likely to result in more successful and prosperous credit unions.

To present this report, the following format is adopted:

Chapter One seeks to contextualise the UK credit union movement. Emphasis is placed on providing descriptive statistics and outlining differences in the profile of credit union penetration within the main UK regions. In this chapter, recent legislative amendments are also considered, as is the debate on the role of UK credit unions as a vehicle for combating financial exclusion.

Chapter Two provides an assessment of the performance of UK credit unions. This performance assessment is based on nine measures linked to the PEARLS financial monitoring and business planning system, as well as efficiency scores estimated using Data Envelopment Analysis (DEA), a technique which is now attracting attention from organisations tasked with regulating and monitoring credit unions. On the basis of this information, credit unions are divided into four groups, ranging from Group One credit unions which are 'strong performers' through to Group Four credit unions which are 'weak performers'. The information is presented for the UK as a whole, then separately for GB and NI. Credit unions in NI are considered separately as they operate under a different legislative framework from credit unions elsewhere in the UK. (To allow comparisons and for completeness, information is presented in the Appendix for credit unions in England and Wales, and Scotland.)

Chapter Three considers new 'fast growth' credit union formations, where the credit union has achieved, in a short period, a significant membership. Two such credit unions are case studied; both are located in England. In analysing these credit unions, an assessment is made of their success to date, the drivers behind their development and whether they can be successful in the long term.

Chapter Four explores merger activity among UK credit unions. Again, a case study format is adopted, with five mergers analysed. These range from a credit union merging with one other credit union to a merger among eight credit unions. In most of the case studies, there was one dominant credit union and the merger essentially occurred as a transfer of engagements into that credit union. Currently, this is the norm among merging UK credit unions. To provide balance and offer findings that can be generalised, one case study considered a merger between two credit unions of broadly equal strength. In considering these mergers, emphasis is placed on the dynamics of the process and whether such mergers are likely to result, in the long term, in more robust, financially sound and successful credit unions. In this chapter, a potential alternative to merging is also case studied. The alternative is where a number of credit unions keep their autonomy but employ a common provider of shared services to help in the management and day-to-day operation of the credit unions.

Having documented the structural characteristics of the UK credit union movement and the ongoing trends within the sector, the analysis in Chapter Five seeks to pinpoint why some credit unions perform better than others. Drawing from Chapter Two, which divided UK credit unions into four differential performing groups, 15 credit unions are chosen for case study. Seven are strong performers, four are average-to-good performers and four are marginal performers. For each of the case investigations, the financial profile of the credit union is assessed, premises and staff are also profiled, the role of volunteers is considered and board structure is examined, including skill sets on the board and the training of directors. Emphasis is placed on identifying the areas where credit unions could improve their performance and the means by which this improvement could be achieved.

The discussion is completed by Chapter Six, which summarises the key issues to emerge from this overview of UK credit unions. Here, we also provide a series of recommendations arising from the results of our study.

UK credit unions (structure, legislation and financial exclusion)

Structure

In excess of 123 million people in 79 nations now belong to a credit union and, in aggregate terms, the assets of credit unions worldwide are calculated at $758 billion (WOCCU, 2003). At the end of 2004, there were 779 credit unions in the UK with a membership of 814,538 and assets of approximately £900 million. This level of membership represents a penetration of less than 1% of the population. In Northern Ireland (NI), the movement is strongest with about 26% of the population belonging to a credit union. The movement in NI has operated for longer – for example, the average age of credit unions in the UK is 15 years; in England and Wales, it is 11 years; in Scotland, it is 12 years while, in NI, it is 23 years (see Ward and McKillop, 2005a, for more details). The movement in NI has also operated under bespoke legislation, and has benefited from a history of strong pioneer support from established organisations such as the Catholic Church and, more recently, the Orange Order. Central/West Scotland has also experienced more success than the rest of Great Britain (GB), accounting for 35% of GB membership.

Table 1 presents some statistics on credit union members, assets and shares per member. This information is presented for four size categories: assets greater than £2 million; assets between £1 million and £2 million; assets between £0.5 million and £1 million; and assets less than £0.5 million. Information is presented for the UK, GB and separately for NI, given that the legislation framework differs and the level of development of the movement is more advanced in this region. (For completeness sake, in the Appendix, similar information is presented separately for credit unions in Scotland and for those in England and Wales.) This tabular information is detailed for credit unions as they stood at the end of 2001. More recent data is not available on individual credit unions because the Financial Services Authority (FSA), which took over the regulation of credit unions in GB in 2002, is prohibited by the 2000 Financial Services and Markets Act from placing detailed information on individual credit unions in the public domain. (It is noted that this contrasts with the situation under the Registry of Friendly Societies, which, up until 2001, provided, on request, detailed data on credit unions in GB. In most other countries, data on individual credit unions are also made available by the lead regulator. For example, in the US, which has 9,300 credit unions, information contained in each credit union's Call Report is made available with a lag of one quarter.)

From Table 1, it can be seen that the majority (75%) of credit unions in the UK are small (assets less than £0.5 million), but the bulk of assets (75%) and members (55%) are to be found in the larger credit unions (assets greater than £2 million), which, in numerical terms, account for only 11% of the sector. It is also evident from the documented statistics that average savings per member rises as credit union size increases, which may suggest that larger credit unions are more able to capture higher income category members.

Comparison of the data for NI credit unions with those in GB immediately highlights that the strength of the UK credit union movement is based in NI, with 73 out of an overall UK total of 95 credit unions with assets in excess of £2 million located in the province. It is also noted that, in each of the size bands, NI credit unions have a higher net worth (saving per member) than credit unions in GB. This may reflect the fact that, in NI, credit unions have been accepted by a more diverse population income mix than in GB. Having made this point, it is also apparent that, in GB, larger scale credit unions have a higher share to member ratio than smaller credit unions, intimating that larger credit unions in GB may also be able to capture a more broad-based income mix of members. It is also the case that between 2001 and 2004 there has been a fall in credit union numbers in GB and, for the most part, this decline has been due to smaller credit unions merging with larger credit unions (see Chapter Four for more details).

Table 1: Summary data by size category (UK, GB, NI), 2001

UK (Assets, A)	A>£2m	£1m<A<£2m	£0.5m<A<£1m	A<£0.5m	Total
Number	95	46	66	628	835
% of total	11.4%	5.5%	7.9%	75.2%	100.0%
Assets (£)	601,072,911	68,230,250	47,811,582	71,484,584	788,599,327
% of total	76.2%	8.7%	6.1%	9.1%	100.0%
Members	392,198	73,756	53,928	177,678	697,560
% of total	56.2%	10.6%	7.7%	25.5%	100.0%
Shares, savings/ member (£)	1,276	804	765	341	948
Great Britain	A>£2m	£1m<A<£2m	£0.5m<A<£1m	A<£0.5m	Total
Number	22	25	35	571	653
% of total	3.4%	3.8%	5.4%	87.4%	100.0%
Assets (£)	143,888,617	34,874,962	24,848,848	59,478,408	263,090,835
% of total	54.7%	13.3%	9.4%	22.6%	100.0%
Members	117,954	46,752	32,834	163,718	361,258
% of total	32.7%	12.9%	9.1%	45.3%	100.0%
Shares, savings/ member (£)	993	664	665	306	609
Northern Ireland	A>£2m	£1m<A<£2m	£0.5m<A<£1m	A<£0.5m	Total
Number	73	21	31	57	182
% of total	40.1%	11.5%	17.0%	31.3%	100.0%
Assets (£)	457,184,294	33,355,288	22,962,734	12,006,176	525,508,492
% of total	87.0%	6.3%	4.4%	2.3%	100.0%
Members	274,244	27,004	21,094	13,960	336,302
% of total	81.5%	8.0%	6.3%	4.2%	100.0%
Shares, savings/ member (£)	1,397	1,047	923	750	1,313

Legislation

Credit unions are governed by internal regulation in conjunction with credit union specific legislation. They are internally regulated by trade associations that provide support and guidance to affiliated credit unions. In 2001, five different trade associations operated within the UK: the Irish League of Credit Unions (ILCU), which is an all-Ireland body with 104 affiliated credit unions located in NI; the Ulster Federation of Credit Unions (UFCU), which had 70 affiliates all in NI (the balance of credit unions in NI, of which there were eight, were either independent or affiliated to the Antigonish model of Nova Scotia); the Association of British Credit Unions (ABCUL) with 515 affiliated credit unions; and the Scottish League of Credit Unions (SLCU) with 45 affiliates[1]. In addition, the remainder of credit unions located in GB were either affiliated to the Association of Independent Credit Unions (AICU) or independent of any trade association.

Hayton (2001) argues that there are essentially two opposing views with respect to the ethos of credit union development and support emanating from trade associations. On the one hand, trade associations such as the UFCU, SLCU and AICU see credit unions as 'small area-based, poverty-alleviating initiatives'. These trade bodies are primarily focused on community development and self-help, with credit union growth being achieved through the formation of new credit unions (Sibbald et al, 2002). In contrast, the ethos of ABCUL and the ILCU, sister trade associations affiliated to the World Council of Credit Unions (WOCCU), is one of monetary scale, scope efficiencies and product expansion. These trade bodies encourage credit unions to grow in size, serve larger areas and adopt professional business approaches to the running of the credit union.

During recent times, the government has endeavoured to develop a framework aimed at broadening the appeal of credit unions. As 'third sector' lenders, they are seen as having an important role to play in providing affordable credit, and many credit unions in GB already operate in areas of significant financial exclusion (HM Treasury, 2005). The start point for recent changes occurred in July 1998, when a Treasury taskforce was established to investigate ways of promoting expansion of the sector in GB. The taskforce report suggested several changes, many of which were phased into operation through legislative revisions to the 1979 Credit Union Act, contained in the 2000 Financial Services and Markets Act and the 2003 Regulatory Reform (Credit Union) Order. The revisions include an increase in the flexibility of the common bond classification; removal of the upper membership limit of 5,000; extensions to allowable loan periods; an introduction of the ability to borrow from other credit unions and authorised banking institutions; permission to charge for ancillary services; and protection of the name 'Credit Union'.

Furthermore, the financial regulation of the sector in GB transferred from the Registry of Friendly Societies to the FSA over the period January 1999 to July 2002. The FSA initiated major changes that would affect the whole sector in GB. A credit union sourcebook, which provides a framework for the regulation and operation of credit unions, was introduced. On an operational level, credit unions can now only be run by suitable approved persons, who must keep proper accounting systems and have adequate financial resources to back their businesses (Ryder, 2001). They can borrow money from sources other than authorised banks and other credit unions, and differentiate between accounts by paying dividends at different rates and more than once a year. The minimum coverage requirement for fidelity bonds has been changed and members are allowed to operate joint accounts (FSA, 2002). The FSA introduced different requirements for two categories of credit union (known as Version 1 and Version 2) that enabled them to undertake deposit-taking. Credit unions qualifying under Version 1 have less strict capital retention requirements, although more restrictive conditions placed on their operations. They can offer small loans over short periods, as well as limited ancillary services, but need permission from the FSA if they wish to take deposits from their

---

[1] As of September 2003, ABCUL had 417 affiliates and the SLCU 41. There was no change in the number of credit unions affiliated to the ILCU and the UFCU.

members. Those credit unions that qualify for Version 2 status can provide larger loans over longer periods of time. They can offer a wider range of ancillary services and have fewer requirements to fulfil in order to be allowed to undertake deposit-taking (FSA, 2001a). At the end of 2004, there were 12 Version 2 credit unions in GB. The FSA's new regime for credit unions also extends to credit union members' funds now being protected by the Financial Services Compensation Scheme. Under the rules of the scheme, eligible depositors receive 100% of the first £2,000 and 90% of the next £33,000, with the maximum amount payable under the scheme to an individual depositor being £31,700. The first credit union to benefit from the scheme was Thameswood Credit Union, located in south-east London. It had 883 members and was closed by the FSA in September 2002 when it was discovered to be heading for insolvency (see Walne, 2002).

In NI, proposals have been put forward for the modernisation of NI policy on credit unions (DETI [NI], 2004). The consultation document poses two fundamental questions about the future direction of the credit union movement in NI. The first is whether credit unions should 'continue to be primarily a local mechanism to address financial inclusion, or should they now aim to be a full service financial cooperative?' (p 25). The second is whether there should be 'active encouragement to developing larger more sophisticated credit unions which are likelier to be more effectively managed, soundly based and have critical mass more capable of delivering a wider and more sophisticated range of financial products?' (p 26). The tenor of the consultation document is that the answer to both questions is in favour of increasing the range of service provision[2]. To that end, the proposals for modernisation suggest removing the membership cap and widening the common bond; increasing the term and size of both savings and loan accounts; requiring credit unions to be part of a savings protection scheme; increasing the services which can be provided by credit unions; the introduction of measures to improve governance, accountability and reporting by credit unions; and broadening the powers available to the Registrar of Friendly Societies.

The legislative amendments which have occurred in GB, and which are proposed for NI, are still viewed in certain quarters as restrictive. This can be argued in relation to the size and term of loans to members and the funds which can be invested by members. Credit unions also face caps on interest rates that can be charged and on dividends that can be paid. It should be noted that the credit union interest rate cap is currently under review for credit unions in GB (HM Treasury, 2005). The consultation document considers a number of scenarios, including the option of increasing the interest rate cap on loans from 1% per month to 2% per month. Restrictions are also placed on who can become a member of a credit union, as the legislation requires that all members belong to a common bond. The common bond or 'common interest' (Berthoud and Hinton, 1989) can be either associational, residential, occupational or 'living and working' (1979 Credit Union Act/1985 Credit Union [NI] Order, as amended by the 1996 Deregulation [Credit Union] Act/ Order). The 2003 Regulatory Reform (Credit Union) Order introduced a further category, which allows the common bond of association to be combined with any of the other classifications.

The purpose of the common bond is to increase the likelihood that members will know each other and, in turn, have a sense of loyalty and commitment to a joint enterprise (Heenan and McLaughlin, 2002). Recently, the FSA has demonstrated a willingness to grant quite extensive common bonds, extending in some cases to become borough-, county- or even nationwide. In the Credit Union sourcebook, the FSA describes the law relating to common bonds. It states that it will interpret the term 'locality' in a broader fashion than the Registry of Friendly Societies did, suggesting that any natural geographic unit or administrative unit comparable in size to the principal tier of local authority in GB – in other words, unitary authorities or county councils

---

[2] Permitting credit unions in NI to broaden the services they offer is becoming increasingly important due to the fall in loan to share ratios. Good practice suggests that this ratio should be in excess of 80%; however, for most credit unions in NI, this ratio is now much lower. In 2001, the loan to share ratio averaged 81% but now (2005) it stands at approximately 55%.

– will be acceptable (CRED 13 Ann 1A G 8[1]-[3]). For employment-based common bonds (when more than one employer is involved), the employees must be employed in a particular 'area'. The FSA have indicated that this term may potentially encompass a much larger space than 'locality', up to the size of a single standard administrative region within GB (CRED 13 Ann 1A G 9). For example, a credit union (Credit Union F in Chapter Four) was granted an occupational common bond that encompasses the whole of England and Wales. While this is the case, it is important to note that, for all types of common bond, where the potential membership is greater than 1 million people, the FSA will operate under the presumption that the common bond is 'so dilute as to be meaningless', and a credit union would have to make a 'particularly strong' argument to convince it otherwise (CRED 13 Ann 1A G 11[3][c]). For potential memberships of less than 100,000, the presumption is in favour of a common bond being present (CRED 13 Ann 1A G 11[3][a]). For potential memberships of between 100,000 and 1 million, there is no presumption in favour of the existence of a common bond, and a credit union must make a 'positive, convincing case' in order to be successful in its application (CRED 13 Ann 1A G 11[3][b]).

Financial exclusion

Fuller (1998) argues that credit unions have the potential to make a partial contribution 'within the geography of financial inclusion'. Fairbairn et al (1997) contend that credit unions' unique characteristics and underlying community self-help ethos provide them with the potential to tackle directly the core aspects of financial exclusion. In particular, the common bond restriction enables credit unions to provide banking facilities and credit to financially excluded members where it would be deemed too risky by mainstream financial institutions (Black and Dugger, 1981). The reason for this is that the committee making the credit assessment belong to the common bond and therefore have knowledge of the character and personal record of each member seeking credit; hence, they can make a quick credit assessment based on the applicant's reputation and savings profile, rather than on their income and assets (Griffiths and Howells, 1991)[3]. This potential has led to a 'long held and popular view' by policy makers that 'credit unions can assist in the tackling of social exclusion' (Mervyn Pedelty, Chief Executive of the Cooperative Bank, in the foreword to Jones [1999]). Particularly in the last two decades, government bodies have supported the credit union movement, regarding it as a tool for combating financial exclusion (McKillop and Wilson, 2003). For example, Lord McIntosh of Haringey opened the debate of the 2003 Regulatory Reform (Credit Union) Order by stating: 'The government support the valuable role credit unions play in tackling financial exclusion and widening access to affordable credit'. *Promoting financial inclusion* (HM Treasury, 2004), published in conjunction with the pre-budget report at the end of 2004, documented the government's financial inclusion priorities of increasing access to banking, to free money advice and to affordable credit. To help achieve these priorities, the government established a Financial Inclusion Taskforce and a Financial Inclusion Fund of £120 million in support of 'the valuable work of credit unions, and to boost the coverage, capacity and sustainability of the sector'. *Promoting financial inclusion* (HM Treasury, 2004) announced that the government would, among other initiatives, set up a growth fund for third sector lenders from within the Financial Inclusion Fund (see HM Treasury, 2005, for more details).

Support by government bodies, including local authorities, to credit unions in GB usually takes the form of direct financial assistance, such as start-up and/or annual revenue grants, or may include non-financial assistance, such as the provision of training, education, facilities (for example, rent-free premises, rate relief, payroll services) and guidance from government-funded credit union

---

[3] It should be noted that a small number of credit unions are at present trialling capacity-based lending. In this instance, the credit union member does not necessarily need to have a savings record with the credit union prior to the granting of a loan. Such a development is perhaps pertinent given the move towards permitting much larger geographic coverage of common bonds. Under such circumstances, it is difficult to envisage a credit union having knowledge of the character and personal record of each member seeking credit.

development workers or development agencies. Jones (1999) suggests that, in the late 1990s, the total annual investment in credit unions in GB was as much as £10-15 million. He found that 80% of community credit unions, 59% of work-based credit unions and 100% of newly registered credit unions from his sample received one-off cash grants when setting up. In addition, 15% of community credit unions, 18% of work-based credit unions and 8% of newly registered credit unions received ongoing cash funding. In that the primary objective of this support is to provide sustainable institutions[4] that are accessible by the financially excluded[5], the emphasis has been on establishing and promoting community-based credit unions located in deprived areas.

To date, however, there has been a general lack of success in establishing sustainable credit unions through these community-based support initiatives, and this has resulted in questions being raised about the effectiveness of credit unions in combating financial exclusion. Debates usually centre around accountability issues; after investing large sums in the movement, policy makers want explanations for the 'lack of success', in terms of overall growth in credit union numbers and the lack of progress towards self-sustainability by individual credit unions.

Many reasons have been forwarded for this slow progress. In a study on the development of the sector in Scotland, research (commissioned by the Scottish Executive) by the Centre for Economic Development and Area Regeneration (2000) concluded that credit unions that start up or operate using the 'ethical approach', which focuses on having a strong community base with much volunteer involvement developing at 'its own pace', have been relatively ineffective. In the periods they considered in their report, few of this type of start-up credit union became self-sustaining. Clutton-Brock (1996) suggests that the stewardship function of a credit union may be an influence in its success. If a credit union is located in a deprived area, stewardship may be provided by persons that do not have the required level of competence or experience. This may make it unattractive to potential members who have higher incomes, thereby restricting the credit union's potential for growth among the poorer sections of the community. Another stumbling block may be the perception held by many that credit unions are 'poor people's banks' (Jones, 1999). This view may restrict the monies that circulate within them to persons on low income. Reifner (1997) argues that this circulation of money among the poor alone is not enough, as circulating the money of the poor within the poor community creates exclusion ghettos. Therefore, to be successful, credit unions need to mobilise the money of the rich as well. In fact, Reifner takes this view further by suggesting that financial cooperatives need to be integrated with larger financial networks to provide the best and most reliable service. Consistent with these views, Ryder (2002) argues that the long-term success of credit unions requires that they attract a wider cross section of people from local communities, not just those who are socially or financially excluded. Donnelly (2002), in more general terms, argues that credit unions in GB continue to perform poorly due to:

> ... unclear goals, confusion as to purpose, government policy and personal animosities
> ... and the split nature of the British movement [which is] split by sector, by size, and by
> nation. (p 8)

In response to some of the issues raised, there has been a gradual shift within the British credit union movement from the ethical/traditional model of credit union development to what has become known as new model credit union development (Jones, 2001). New model development is based on seven doctrines of success – serving the financial needs of the population at large, maximising

---

[4] Credit union sustainability is described by Hayton (2001) as being financially independent, having the ability to cover all costs including 'fidelity bond insurance, bad debt reserves, premises, volunteer expenses, staff salaries, marketing, training, rates, lighting, utilities, etc' (p 282).

[5] Hayton et al (2005) suggest that, if credit unions are to make a greater contribution to fighting financial exclusion, then they need to be more flexible in their lending practices, in particular relaxing their rule that members can only borrow after they have first saved. However, if this is done, then the risk of bad debts is likely to increase. Accordingly, it is proposed that loan guarantee funds be considered to underwrite loans.

savings, portfolio diversification, operating efficiency, financial discipline, self-governance and assimilation (Jones, 2004). Evidence of the acceptance of this new model can be seen in ABCUL's promotion of more business-orientated approaches to credit union development. It can also be seen in the trend by the FSA of permitting common bonds which are county-, borough- or nationwide. It is also witnessed in the formation of some new 'fast growth' credit unions, which are heavily grant-aided by their local authority, and, from the outset, have bespoke premises and a professional management team, adopt capacity-based lending and attempt to pay a dividend early on. (Two newly formed 'fast growth' credit unions are case studied in Chapter Three.) Only with the passage of time can a true and fair judgement be made as to the success of this policy shift in GB away from the traditional/ethical model of credit union development to the new model approach. Having made this point, it is worthwhile to note that credit unions in NI are functioning well and that they remain structured around a strong community base, encourage volunteer involvement and tend to develop at their own pace. Ward and McKillop (2005b), in an overview of subsidisation in NI credit unions note, for example, that large credit unions (assets greater than £2 million) are in general located in the most deprived areas in NI, benefit from just over one quarter of their total labour requirement being provided by volunteers, typically own their own premises and receive no subsidisation of day-to-day operational costs, with only three credit unions in 2005 receiving grant income to help in the purchase of fixed assets.

2

Performance measurement

In this chapter, two different approaches are utilised to assess the performance of UK credit unions. In the first instance, nine measures are computed with each exploring a different aspect of the operational structure of credit unions. Table 2 details each of the measures and presents a rationale as to why the measure in question is calculated. These performance metrics are in part drawn from the PEARLS monitoring and supervisory framework. Each letter of the PEARLS acronym stands for a key area of credit union operations; these are Protection, Effective financial structure, Asset quality, Rates of return and cost, Liquidity and Signs of growth (see Richardson, 2002, for details of PEARLS).

A PEARLS pilot project has recently been undertaken with 20 credit unions in Great Britain (GB) funded by Barclays Bank and the Office of the Deputy Prime Minister, (see ABCUL, 2004, which provides detailed material on the nine community-based credit unions involved in the pilot study). Since 2002, the Irish League of Credit Unions (ILCU) has calculated, on a quarterly basis, PEARLS for its member credit unions.

The second assessment procedure employed in this chapter is Data Envelopment Analysis (DEA). DEA is a relative performance assessment framework where credit unions, depending on their relative strength, are allocated a value between 1 and 0. Credit unions with a score of 1 are highly efficient, with efficiency defined as the ratio of outputs produced to inputs consumed, and cannot increase their services without an increase in resources. Credit unions with scores of less than 1 have potential to improve their efficiency. The lower the score, the greater the room for improvement.

Burger (1993, p 1) argues that DEA '… goes beyond traditional, over simplistic ratios that fail to recognize the unique member-oriented service characteristics and structures of credit unions. It provides a method of simultaneously evaluating the impact of multiple outputs in a complex financial services environment.'

DEA is, in essence, a sophisticated quantitative approach that can be used to create efficiency measures for credit unions in order to identify and rank strong performing and weaker credit unions. Detailed discussion of a DEA estimating framework applied to UK credit unions can be found in McKillop et al, 2002. Fried and Lovell (1993) use DEA to explore the relative efficiency of US credit unions. Worthington (1998) and Brown et al (1997) use DEA to explore the efficiency of small cross sectional samples of credit unions in Australia. McKillop et al (2002) use DEA to investigate the cost performance of UK credit unions using radial and non-radial efficiency measures. Pille and Paradi (2002) employ four different DEA models to detect weaknesses in credit unions in Ontario, Canada.

The nine performance measures (see Table 2) and the DEA score are both based on end 2001 data, the latest date for which complete information is available for all UK credit unions. As noted earlier, more recent data are not available on individual credit unions because the Financial Services Authority (FSA), which took over the regulation of credit unions in GB in 2002, is prohibited from providing detailed information on individual credit unions.

Table 2: Performance measures

Measure	Rationale
Members	Success for CUs may be most basically defined by the attraction of members. This is because there is no profit motive; simply by attracting members, CUs are achieving part of their social goal(s).
Member change	This represents the success of a CU in attracting/retaining members from year to year, and represents a proxy for the operational success of the CU's marketing/member satisfaction performance.
Shares/members	This is a key input for CUs, as they will be unable to lend to potential borrowers without sufficient savings. If this measure increases, it is a sign that the CU's members are happy to continue to invest their funds in the CU.
Loans/shares	This is a measure of the CU's success in attracting borrowers. By doing this, it fulfils social goals (by providing a source of credit to members).
Operating expenses/ operating income	This is a measure of efficiency. This measure is calculated to compare operating income with operating expenses, on a like-for-like basis. The lower the measure, the better.
Loan delinquency/average loans*	This will be a determinant of the return available for distribution to members. If it is high, year after year, this could threaten the viability of the CU, and indicates poor management loan policy/collection operations.
Net interest received/ average loans	If this is low (compared to market rates), it is providing a direct financial benefit for current members, as well as possibly being attractive to potential members
(Interest+dividends+ retentions)/(savings+ shareholdings+capital) ie Return/average member funds	This is a return to members. It is a measure of the financial benefit of saving in the CU, and should also indicate the potential of the CU in attracting savers. The higher it is, the better.
Capital/assets	Generally speaking, the higher this ratio is, the more successful a CU can be thought to be. While the exact percentage of desirable capital may not be theoretically derivable, it is clear that some capital is desirable, to assuage the effects of volatility in 'earnings'.

Note: *The delinquency data is not available for NI; hence we calculated the alternative measure Loan Provisions/ Average Loans.

In Table 3, averages of the nine performance measures are presented for the UK, GB and NI. As earlier, it was decided to present separately for NI credit unions as they operate under a marginally different legislative framework and are somewhat more advanced than credit unions elsewhere in the UK. Information is presented separately for credit unions in Scotland and in England and Wales in the Appendix. For each of the measures, an overall statistic is reported plus a statistic for each of four groups. The groups are determined on the basis of a relative ranking on all the ratios calculated. An equal number of credit unions are allocated to each of the groups. Dividing the sector into quartiles is not an empirically based definition; rather, it is a useful means of breaking up the continuum of credit union performance. Group One credit unions are the best performers, on the basis of the relative ranking constructed from the nine measures; Group Four credit unions are the worst performers, and Groups Two and Three lie between these two extremes.

Table 3: Selection of performance measures (UK, GB, NI), 2001

UK	Group 1	Group 2	Group 3	Group 4	Overall
Members	2,197	635	332	174	835
Member change	8.32%	12.33%	14.38%	0.37%	9.19%
Shares/member (£)	1,190	594	391	242	948
Loans/shares	87.15%	78.97%	79.64%	57.56%	85.33%
Operating expenditure/ operating income	28.41%	56.55%	87.27%	166.28%	35.01%
Loan provisions/average loans	1.81%	3.18%	5.52%	7.43%	2.15%
Net interest received/average loans	10.46%	11.15%	11.48%	11.51%	10.59%
Return/average members' funds	5.53%	3.49%	1.86%	0.09%	5.09%
Capital/assets	11.04%	8.21%	4.36%	3.82%	10.35%
Great Britain	**Group 1**	**Group 2**	**Group 3**	**Group 4**	**Overall**
Members	1,356	449	246	156	553
Member change	14.0%	15.3%	13.6%	−3.8%	12.7%
Shares/member (£)	805	399	282	238	625
Loans/shares	98.6%	85.0%	68.8%	56.3%	94.2%
Operating expenditure/ operating income	39.7%	82.5%	150.1%	180.9%	51.4%
Delinquent loans/average loans	2.3%	9.1%	18.9%	19.2%	3.9%
Loan provisions/average loans	1.4%	3.8%	5.8%	7.7%	1.9%
Net interest received/average loans	10.9%	10.9%	10.9%	11.9%	10.9%
Return/average members' funds	6.1%	2.7%	2.4%	0.8%	5.3%
Capital/assets	10.0%	7.0%	5.3%	2.6%	9.2%
Northern Ireland	**Group 1**	**Group 2**	**Group 3**	**Group 4**	**Overall**
Members	3,589	1,924	1,092	746	1,848
Member change	5.71%	5.34%	4.67%	7.25%	5.61%
Shares/member (£)	1,485	1,341	1,020	818	1,313
Loans/shares	83.75%	80.29%	74.43%	72.78%	81.08%
Operating expenditure/ operating income	23.20%	28.24%	33.07%	36.56%	26.41%
Loan provisions/average loans	1.71%	2.53%	3.45%	5.09%	2.30%
Net interest received/average loans	9.78%	10.65%	11.03%	11.74%	10.25%
Return/average members' funds	5.61%	4.81%	4.33%	3.12%	5.10%
Capital/assets	11.47%	10.74%	10.15%	7.97%	10.92%

Two general points of note emerge from Table 3. First, credit unions in NI are much more robust financial organisations than are to be found elsewhere in the UK. Groups One, Two and Three in NI appear to comprise relatively strong credit unions. It is only in the case of Group Four that questions should be raised as to the strength and soundness of the credit unions. Most notable with respect to this group is that the capital base (7.97%) is less than the regulatory norm, bad debt provision (at 5.09%) is high, there is a weakness in transforming members' shareholdings to loans (72.78%), the return enjoyed by fund-providing members (2.62%) is somewhat poor and, in general, these credit unions are less wealthy, with shareholding per member of £818.

Second, in the case of credit unions in GB, there are undoubted questions to be asked about the long-term viability of credit unions identified as belonging to Groups Three and Four, and perhaps even some Group Two credit unions. Average size, as measured by members, is 246 for Group Three and only 156 for Group Four. Shares per member are also small at £282 and £238 for Group Three and Group Four respectively. Perhaps much more worryingly for these two groups of credit unions is their level of delinquent loans and their capital strength. For Group Three credit unions, delinquent loans as a percentage of total loans were 18.9% while capital adequacy was 5.3%. The comparable figures for Group Four credit unions were 19.2% and 2.6% respectively. Information is also detailed in Table 3 on operating expenses as a proportion of income. This measure has been computed by excluding items which can be influenced by accounting adjustments, such as depreciation, bad debt provisions, tax and non-standard items such as 'other income'. If this ratio exceeds 100%, it may point to the presence of subsidisation. The reported figures in Table 3 of 150.1% and 180.9% for Group Three and Group Four credit unions respectively very much suggests that, without subsidisation, these credit unions would, for the most part, not be viable.

In general, Table 3 suggests that 75% of credit unions in NI are relatively strong and robust. However, in GB there is a question mark over the long-term survival of at least 50% of credit unions. Indeed, as highlighted in the introductory comments, a process of contraction in credit union numbers is now under way. In England and Wales, the total number of credit unions fell by 55 between 2003 and 2004, although this number underestimates the true decline as it does not control for new credit union establishment during the same period. For the most part, those credit unions that have disappeared have tended to be the smaller and financially weak Group Three and Group Four credit unions. Interestingly, during the same period, credit union numbers in Scotland only fell by three, while there was no change in the more financially robust sector in NI.

Table 4 details the relative efficiency characteristics of credit unions, with efficiency computed using DEA. In this study, a two input (management and non-management expenses plus dividends paid), three output (loans, shares and cash plus investments) model was utilised. Three different populations are considered in the computation of these efficiency scores. In the first instance, the population set is all UK credit unions. Computer programs are then re-run to separately assess the relative efficiency of credit unions in GB and then the relative efficiency of credit unions in NI. (Information is presented in the Appendix on the DEA scores of credit unions in England and Wales and in Scotland.)

Consider first of all the component of Table 4 which addresses the relative efficiency of credit unions in NI. The average efficiency score was 0.75. This suggests that credit unions in NI could on average potentially produce the same level of output with approximately a 25% equiproportionate reduction in all input expenditures. Out of 182 credit unions in NI in 2001, a total of 30 were classified as efficient (efficient score = 1). From that number of efficient credit unions, 21 were identified as 'peer' credit unions, which implies that these credit unions are earmarked as role model credit unions for other credit unions identified as inefficient.

For comparison purposes, the four groups detailed in Table 4 are those that were utilised in Table 3. It is clear that a commonality exists between the financial ratio analysis and DEA. For example, the average efficiency score increases from 0.6418 to 0.8765 as we move from Group Four credit unions to Group One. It is noticeable that a large number of the DEA-identified efficient credit unions (13 out of the 30) are classified as Group One credit unions (of which 12 are 'peers').

Finally with regard to credit unions in NI, a sizeable number appear to be subject to decreasing returns to scale – in other words, an increase in efficiency could be achieved through downsizing. This result is not oversurprising as in 2001 these credit unions operated within narrowly defined boundaries as to the type, amount and range of products they could offer to their members. Many of these credit unions have invested in premises, staff and technology, and have the untapped potential of offering a wider range and longer term product portfolio. Consequently, it is of little surprise that they are classed as being subject to decreasing returns to scale. Recent and anticipated legislative

Table 4: Data envelopment analysis (DEA), (UK, GB, NI), 2001

UK DEA	Group 1	Group 2	Group 3	Group 4	Overall
Efficiency score	0.5547	0.3703	0.2918	0.1914	0.3522
Efficient CUs (number of)	11	7	8	0	26
CUs with peers	8	4	7	0	19
Total peer count	1,817	437	554	0	2,808
DRS (Number subject to)	206	199	190	170	765
IRS (Number subject to)	1	7	15	33	56
GB DEA	**Group 1**	**Group 2**	**Group 3**	**Group 4**	**Overall**
Efficiency score	0.5746	0.3528	0.2885	0.2484	0.3410
Efficient CUs (number of)	10	8	2	0	20
CUs with peers	7	8	1	0	16
Total peer count	1,040	942	56	0	2,038
DRS (Number subject to)	159	149	145	122	575
IRS (Number subject to)	3	7	16	38	64
NI DEA	**Group 1**	**Group 2**	**Group 3**	**Group 4**	**Overall**
Efficiency score	0.8765	0.7679	0.7111	0.6418	0.7501
Efficient CUs (number of)	13	4	4	9	30
CUs with peers	12	3	3	5	23
Total peer count	391	89	41	98	619
DRS (Number subject to)	45	45	42	38	170
IRS (Number subject to)	0	0	2	5	7

changes permitting the provision of higher value services to members may justify the current levels of expenditure and push credit unions towards constant returns and hence efficient operating size.

Turning to the other component parts of Table 4, it is evident that the documented level of inefficiency is much higher. For the UK as a whole, the average efficiency score is 0.3522, compared with 0.341 for credit unions in GB. These numbers suggest that there is the potential for producing the same output levels using almost a 65% input reduction.

In terms of efficient credit unions (efficiency score = 1), there are 20 such credit unions for the GB analysis, of which 16 are 'peers' (26 for the UK component, of which 19 are 'peers'). Broad uniformity exists as to those credit unions identified as efficient in the GB and UK analysis. Thirteen English and Welsh credit unions are classified as efficient in the UK analysis, with 11 of these also efficient in the GB component. (Nine credit unions located in NI were highlighted as efficient in the UK analysis, with six of these also identified as 'peer' credit unions.)

It is, again, also notable that for both the GB and UK aspects of Table 4, the average efficiency score and, indeed, the number of credit unions identified as efficient increase as we move from Group Four credit unions through to Group One credit unions. However, irrespective of the group considered, there is a high level of inefficiency within the credit union movement in GB. The average efficiency score is 0.2484 for Group Four rising to 0.5746 for Group One. Therefore, the most efficient group – Group One – can still achieve efficiency savings of 43%, while Group Four credit unions can, on average, save 75% of their current expenditure on inputs and still produce the same output levels.

Furthermore, in Table 4, it can also be seen that credit unions identified as scale inefficient are invariably classified as being subject to decreasing returns. Again, this emphasises that a level of investment in premises, staff and equipment has taken place which is not warranted in terms of the range and volume of financial services that are being provided by credit unions.

This analysis of nine financial measures and DEA efficiency scores emphasises that there is a degree of weakness in the UK credit union movement, particularly those credit unions located in England and Wales and in Scotland, with a question mark over the long-term survival of at least 50% of credit unions in GB. While structural weakness does also exist for credit unions in NI, the degree of incidence is less pronounced than is the case for credit unions in GB. Donnelly (2002) argues that the closure of many small credit unions can be expected to benefit the movement in GB in a number of ways:

> It is essential that if credit unions are to prosper that the number of (credit) unions is reduced dramatically.... The closure of many small credit unions will impact on the security and growth of the movement in three ways. First it will create better, safer and bigger credit unions. Second it will enable the trade bodies to concentrate on the development needs of fewer credit unions and so perform better. Third it will improve the quality of service and product range that (credit) unions can offer. (p 14)

3
Newly formed 'fast growth' credit unions

The performance assessment of credit unions detailed in Chapter Two was primarily based on 2001 data. Consequently, credit unions formed during and after 2001 were not included as part of the analysis. In total, there have been 54 new formations in the intervening period (30 in 2002, 8 in 2003 and 16 in 2004). Some of these credit unions have experienced significant membership expansion and, if they were assessed on membership size alone, they would unequivocally be categorised as strong performing Group One credit unions (see Table 3). For other measures, such as capital strength, sufficient time has not yet elapsed to permit these credit unions to accumulate the requisite level of institutional capital. For many of these new start, 'fast growth' credit unions, their capital to assets ratio will be of a similar magnitude to that of weak performing Group Four credit unions (see Table 3). Although no time span is framed in legislation for UK credit unions to have in place adequate levels of capital, guidance from other movements suggests that 5-10 years is the normal expectation. For example, US credit unions are expected to have a net worth ratio of between 0% and 1.99% within 3 years; 2-3.49% within 5 years; 3.5-5.99% within 7 years and 6-6.99% within 10 years. US credit unions with a net worth of between 6% and 6.99% are deemed to be adequately capitalised.

To investigate why these new formations have occurred and the factors driving their strong membership growth, two new start, 'fast growth' credit unions were case studied. Both credit unions were based in England. Indeed, more generally, the majority of new formations have been in England. For example, of the 16 newly registered credit unions in 2004, 13 were in England and three were in Scotland, with no new credit unions being established in Northern Ireland (NI) or Wales. (Comparable figures for 2003 are seven in England, one in Scotland and, again, no new establishments in NI or Wales.)

Credit Union A was established towards the end of 2000. As of March 2005, it had almost 3,000 members with a further 250 juvenile members. Its assets totalled £1.4 million, with a loan to share ratio of 55% and shares per member of £450. The credit union paid a dividend for the first time in 2004 amounting to 1%. Its common bond is 'live or work' and encompasses an inner city borough with a potential membership of 300,000. The credit union operates out of three branches in the borough, with the most recent branch opening in 2005. It has 5.5 full-time equivalent employees with staff costs, at the end of 2004, of approximately £120,000.

The objective in this relatively newly formed credit union of having a cohort of salaried staff plus a 'network' of branches was to fast track membership and asset growth. A board member of the credit union in question suggested that this format is increasingly common for credit unions in Great Britain (GB):

> "It was intended from the beginning that we have professional staff ... and as far as I can see most of the 'live or work' community credit unions seem to be starting up the

same way, unless they already have a history and are, say, transforming themselves from a council credit union into a broader based credit union."

In order to increase the credit union's attractiveness to new members, the credit union is presently moving from a loans policy based on a multiple of savings to capacity-based lending – in other words, loans based on the member's ability to meet the debt obligations:

"Up to now we have been working on borrowing a multiple of savings but now we are moving quickly towards capacity-based lending. That can obviously make a difference in terms of attracting members because we can basically lend immediately."

In conjunction with this shift towards capacity-based lending, the credit union has also begun to utilise PEARLS. It was noted that, through PEARLS, issues surrounding the credit union's capitalisation were coming to the fore (at present institutional capital as a percentage of total assets is less than 2%). However, it was also noted that the credit union considered weak capitalisation a price worth paying for rapid membership growth:

"If we look at the PEARLS we run close to the wind in terms of capitalisation and so forth ... it's an intention ... the objective is to grow fast and develop, not to necessarily be as conservative perhaps as traditionally credit unions have been."

The ability of the credit union to hire staff and operate a 'network' of branches is due to its attracting various grants and subsidies: "We're dependent on getting going as fast as we have through various kind of subsidies and fundings and some gifts from corporates."

For the year ending September 2004, the credit union received in excess of £100,000 in grants, having previously received approximately £70,000 in 2003 and £100,000 in 2002. This funding has in large part been obtained from the borough council and has been triggered by the job creation role of the credit union, but more importantly by the credit union's role in the promotion of social inclusion. As part of its mission, the credit union views as a priority the provision of saving and borrowing facilities to those who are unemployed or on very low incomes.

The credit union considers that after seven or eight years of operation it will be self-sustaining. However, it is at present searching for additional sources of grant income.

Credit Union B was established in 2003. It has five employees who are now all directly employed by the credit union, although a number were initially employed by the borough council with their role, in conjunction with the council's social regeneration unit, that of actually establishing the credit union. The credit union has two branches, with the second branch opened during 2005.

As of May 2005, the credit union had approximately 2,500 members, of whom 400 were juvenile members. The credit union's common bond is 'live or work' and it embraces a potential membership of 600,000. The credit union's membership growth has been achieved in part by targeting those who might otherwise be considered as financially excluded. A representative of Credit Union B stated:

"We have been proactive in opening accounts for people on benefits. One of the key things happening at present is the government arranging for benefits to be paid direct rather than cheques, so that in the last three months we have opened 250 accounts for people on Jobseeker's Allowance."

It should also be emphasised that part of the service agreement for obtaining grant income from the council via, for example, the Neighbourhood Renewal Fund is dependent on the credit unions reaching out to those who are financially excluded.

As of September 2004, Credit Union B had approximately £620,000 in assets, a loan to share ratio of 54% and shares per member of approximately £290.

Credit Union B has not as yet embraced PEARLS nor capacity-based lending. The credit union requires members to save for a three-month period, with loans then available as a multiple of three times savings up to a maximum of £10,000. In justifying this more traditional approach to lending, the manager of the credit union, who previously was an area manager for a high street bank, argued:

> "I like what we are doing at the moment because there is that commitment to save to start with ... to move into capacity-based lending starts to strike of credit scoring applications like the banks do.... To lend in this environment, it is a great deal of trust ... establishing things that you can't put on the computer as to an individual's circumstances. I personally feel that we should keep away from looking too much like a bank."

Credit Union B is very heavily grant dependent, with the manager estimating that in year one start-up costs were of the magnitude of £250,000. The 2004 annual report indicates that grants of £127,458 were received in 2003, with this figure rising to £206,911 in 2004. The funding is channelled to the credit union through the borough council's social regeneration unit and is utilised to support the credit union's work in the area of financial inclusion, as well as its role of providing work experience and volunteering, reflecting "its aspirations and ethos as a social enterprise and community business".

The manager of Credit Union B argued that the credit union was an ideal vehicle to help those who might otherwise face financial exclusion and, in that context, more than justified the initial investment amounts:

> "To spend initially £250,000 to £300,000 [on the credit union] which at this stage has 2,500 members with the potential to increase further is money well spent. I have only to look at the volume of money spent on advice centres which don't have to have an end product. We have a facility that allows them to budget. We have a facility which allows them to pay in their salaries, keep their benefits. We have a facility which allows them to borrow at non-extortionate rates. So what we provide at the end of the day would be seen as fairly good in comparison to the funding we get."

The business plan of Credit Union B suggests that the credit union can become self-sufficient in six or seven years. It anticipates that self-sufficiency is achievable when the credit union has £9 million in assets, 7,000 members and a loan to share ratio of 70%. Given the present pace of membership growth, the target of 7,000 members should be met. More problematic is the goal of achieving £9 million in assets. This will require the credit union to broaden its appeal to include both the financially excluded and salaried members. Also problematic for this credit union is that it is significantly undercapitalised with a capital to assets ratio of less than 1%.

Final comments on newly formed credit unions

The two credit unions case studied are in part byproducts of initiatives by local councils in the area of financial inclusion. A 'hothouse' approach has been utilised to establish and develop both credit unions. Key aspects of the approach include the initial project team being organised by the council, the provision of substantive grant income and the employment from the outset of a professional management team to run the credit union. To date, impressive results have been achieved by both credit unions, particularly in terms of membership growth.

This hothouse approach contrasts with the traditional/ethical, volunteer-focused evolutionary process of credit union establishment and development. Although the latter approach is more protracted, it has the advantage that the credit union board in the formative years will be involved in the day-to-day operation of the credit union. This encourages ownership as well as hands-on knowledge of the credit union's operational requirements. This issue of the board knowing what the credit union was about, and taking ownership, was an issue exercising the management team of Credit Union B:

> "The only drawback in terms of the way we were set up is the quality of my board, because they have never experienced what it is like to grow. In the past, in the old style, the volunteers were those that actually ran the credit union. They would be in there on a Monday morning opening up and serving the first few customers. This credit union has never been in that position given the way it has been set up, having paid staff from the outset. So if I could change something it would be that they [the board] would run the credit union before getting paid staff. They have to take ownership."

Both credit unions are presently concerned, and rightly so, with providing a service to those who might otherwise face financial exclusion. The longer term success of both credit unions is, however, critically dependent on attracting a cross section of members from their local communities. As previously highlighted, Reifner (1997) argues that circulating the money of the poor within the poor community creates exclusion ghettos. To be successful in the long term, credit unions must mobilise the money of the rich as well.

Both credit unions have been heavily pump-primed through grant aid and, although both have business plans which target sustainability after six to seven years, it is perhaps apposite to note that the international evidence suggests that dependency on donor funds undermines self-sufficiency and effective performance (Jones, 2003). With reference to UK credit unions, McKillop and Wilson (2003) note that dependency on external grants and subsidy can lead to a lack of entrepreneurship in credit unions. Jones (2003), based on case study analysis of credit unions in the West Midlands, also notes that the termination of grants and subsidies can present credit unions with immense organisational and operational difficulties.

For these reasons, it is important that the business plan projections regarding sustainability materialise. And in this context it was somewhat disconcerting that the manager of Credit Union B should hold the belief that:

> "… once you are involved with the borough they will find it very hard to see us go under. If I didn't have the funding in place I probably would get the money because they were behind this venture in the first place."

4

Case study analysis of UK credit union mergers

Examining the dynamics involved in mergers among UK credit unions entails consideration of a range of complex factors. This chapter examines, through the detailed analysis of a series of in-depth case studies of credit union mergers, the range of drivers identified in recent merger activity. Selection of credit unions as objects of a case study investigation was done on a random basis, although geographical coverage was considered important, which resulted, therefore, in one case study being based in Scotland, Wales and Northern Ireland (NI) respectively, with the balance of case studies being located in England. In terms of the performance classification reported in Chapter Two, two case studies involved weak performing Group Four credit unions, two case studies focused on credit unions drawn from the average performing Group Two and one case study involved a credit union drawn from the strong performing Group One. Interviews were conducted with board members and management from both the acquiring and acquired credit unions. In order to ensure anonymity of the credit unions taking part in the case studies, they are referred to in the later discussion simply by alphabetical letter. Table 5 provides a summary of the dates of mergers and the trade affiliations, assets and membership of the case study credit unions.

The case study credit unions are mostly community-based credit unions. One exception is the very large employee-based credit union located in the north of England (Credit Union F). The Welsh credit union (Credit Union D) started as a public sector employee-based credit union but has become, through a process of mergers involving smaller credit unions, a city-wide community-based credit union. The Scottish credit union (Credit Union C) is one of the largest community-based credit unions in Scotland and is located in an economically depressed area in the west of Scotland. The credit union located in NI (Credit Union E) is the only independent credit union in our sample; the other credit unions belong to ABCUL. The credit union in NI serves a localised community in West and North Belfast. The remaining credit union, Credit Union G, is located in East London. Credit Union G started as a public sector employee-based credit union but has now shifted its common bond to a community-based one.

Theoretical perspectives and empirical evidence on credit union mergers

Before looking at the results from the case study investigations, it is appropriate to map out briefly key theoretical perspectives on mergers, especially where this relates to credit unions. Within a competitive financial services sector, there appears to be a relentless pressure on providers of financial services to increase their efficiency and attract new customers by increasing their geographical reach and the range of products they offer. Therefore, mergers are seen as instrumental in improving efficiency, whereby both economies of scale and scope might be achieved. In terms of UK credit unions, McKillop et al (2002), in a study of their efficiency, note that UK credit unions suffer from a considerable degree of scale inefficiency, with in excess of 50% of inefficient credit unions subject to decreasing returns of scale (see also Chapter Two). This indicates, however, that these credit unions' efficiency may be increased by either reducing their size or relaxing regulatory constraints on

Table 5: Assets and membership of dominant credit unions and merging credit unions

Dominant CU* assets and membership before merger	Merger dates	Type of merging CU**	Assets of merging credit union	Membership of merging credit union***
Credit Union C (G2) £4.6m 5,185	2002	Community	£498,288	649
Credit Union D (G4) £0.87m 1,463	2000	Community	£9,469	61
	2001	Community	£28,941	257
	2001	Community	£19,409	198
	2001	Community	£17,834	n/a
	2001	Community	£25,463	106
	2001	Community	£29,397	133
	2001	Community	£31,427	117
	2001	Community	£32,600	151
	2001	Community	£79,744	508
Credit Union E (G2) £1.3m 2,408	1999	Community	£421,398	1,072
	2001	Community	£417,016	1,410
	2001	Community	£149,619	206
Credit Union F (G1) £30.5m 9,961	2004	Employee	£6,200,000	4,300
Credit Union G (G4) £1.75m 1,692	1997	Employee	£92,313	200
	1997	Community	£49,357	138
	2001	Community	£771,560	3,194

Notes:

*All the dominant credit unions are affiliated to ABCUL with the exception of Credit Union E, which is independent.

**All the merging credit unions were affiliated to ABCUL with the exception of the credit unions that merged with Credit Union E; these were affiliated to the UFCU.

***Note the membership figure here is members on the books; the actual active membership that transfers as a result of a merger is often lower.

the services they are able to provide. Currently, these credit unions operate within narrowly defined boundaries as to the type and range of products they can offer to their members. Larger credit unions have invested heavily in premises, staff and technology and many are classed as being subject to decreasing returns to scale. If credit unions are able to cross-sell higher value services to their members, then the current levels of investment in premises, staff and technology may prove justified.

There is no agreed unitary theory of mergers. Some major theoretical perspectives on mergers draw on paradigms based purely on the outlook of neoclassical economics, although it is unlikely that this model is capable of providing a compelling rationale for credit union mergers. The reason for this is that, under perfect competition and perfect costless information, maximising firms will all simply adopt the most efficient technology, removing the need to merge (Collins, 2003). If the perfect competition assumption is dropped, mergers may be rational if increased market share allows profits to be increased. This seems inappropriate for credit unions as they are not necessarily maximising profits, and the size of any one credit union is small compared to the size of the financial services markets in the UK, meaning it is implausible that increasing market share through merger would precipitate the exercise of market power. Finally, if the assumption of perfect costless information is relaxed, mergers may occur because of information asymmetry, or agency problems; in other words, managers owning less than 100% of the entity they work for may embark on mergers that maximise their utility while not necessarily maximising the benefits to the owners of the entity. Collins points out that this leads to a situation of 'anything goes', meaning that, even though a merger may not appear to make sense, it must be rational (from the manager's perspective) because of the assumptions of the model. Her view is that neoclassical economics cannot offer an explanation for the cause of mergers other than 'manager knows best'. In contrast, other perspectives draw on New Institutional Economics (NIE). Here, theory allows for the existence of costly transaction costs and for bounded rationality. Under this assumption, people are assumed to behave rationally but to make choices on the basis of imperfect information, meaning an ex post analysis of a particular decision may appear irrational to an observer in possession of superior information. For instance, NIE posits 'that agents produce a range of formal and informal institutions to reduce transaction costs' (Collins, 2003, p 990). In effect, 'institutions are the structure that human beings impose on human interaction' (North, 2000, p 37). Under NIE, individuals deliberately produce institutions in order to promote maximisation and reduce risk; they never arise unintentionally, or through chaos. Both these different perspectives clearly emphasise underlying rational economic behaviour as the key to explaining merger activity.

Paradigms based on rational behaviour, although fairly dominant in approaches to the study of mergers, do not exist unchallenged. For instance, Institutional Economics (IE) differs vastly from the first two frameworks mentioned earlier. This perspective does not, for instance, assume that individuals and/or firms are maximising:

> Individuals (and institutions) are fallible; learning and individual action may have unintended consequences for other individuals within the firm, for the firm itself, or for the individual who initiated the change. An action set in motion will have effect, but the effect will vary according to the agency of the individuals involved and the institutions evoked. (Collins, 2003, p 994)

The effect of this is that firms are a hodgepodge of different institutions; combining two does not result in the simple 'sum' of the originals. They may interact in unexpected ways in order to produce the institutions of the new organisation. Under IE, there can be no general explanation for mergers; each one must be examined individually by an (historic) evaluation of the evolution of each organisation. This will encompass factors such as technology, finance, ideology, the role of labour, unions, powerful individuals and groups, and legislative frameworks. (Roe, 1993) The effect of this is that IE is not useful in explaining the reason why a merger occurred unless the merging institutions are studied in detail, which is obviously not going to be feasible a lot of the time. Collins suggests that IE is 'rather better' at examining the consequences of mergers than providing a theory of the reasons for their occurrence.

Mergers have been, historically, extremely prevalent in the more advanced credit union systems found in the US, Australia and Canada. Over 4,700 credit unions were involved in mergers in the US between 1990 and 1995 (Fried at al, 1999). Chmura Economics and Analytics (2004) note that, in the US, the number of mergers among federally insured credit unions has decreased over the 1990-2002 period. From 1990 through 2002, an average of 324 credit unions merged each year. During the first five years of the period, an average of 405 credit unions merged each year compared with an average of 282 over the last five years of the period. In Australia, the population of credit unions fell from 342 to 245 between 1992 and 1998, and Ralston et al (2001) state that 'the decline [was] caused almost exclusively by mergers' (p 2278). Both studies cited present evidence on the relative benefits to acquirers and acquirees involved in mergers, and on the characteristics of successful mergers. In Canada, similar rationalisation of credit union numbers has occurred through mergers, and between 1970 and 2004 the number of credit unions in Canada reduced from 7,000 to 600.

Comparison of the major US and Australian studies of credit union mergers, conducted by Fried et al (1999) and Ralston et al (2001) respectively, reveals some interesting findings. It should be noted that Fried et al (1999) use a much larger sample than Ralston et al (2001): 1,654 US merger participants between 1988 and 1995, compared to 31 Australian mergers between 1993 and 1995. However, Ralston et al (2001), in contrast to Fried et al (1999), also include a control group of non-merging credit unions to address the question as to whether efficiency gains for merged credit unions are greater than those achieved by credit unions that grow without merger. The Fried et al (1999) study on mergers finds some post-acquisition service improvements in target firms, but no change, on average, among acquirers. They find that about 50% of acquirers and 20-50% of targets suffer a decline in service after a consolidation. Additionally, acquired credit unions are likely to benefit from mergers if they have room to improve in the form of weak loan portfolios and high returns on assets (ROAs), allowing acquiring managers to improve the lending operation and reallocate the high ROAs. Similarly, acquiring credit unions are likely to benefit if they have previous experience with mergers and select employee groups. (Select employee groups are businesses that enter into an arrangement with a credit union that allows their employees to become members of the credit union.) Finally, Fried et al (1999) conclude that merger partners are likely to benefit if they are different, as size differences minimise disruption and other types of diversity create synergies.

The Australian study conducted by Ralston et al (2001) found that technical and scale efficiency gains were found for some of the acquirers and acquirees but that, for an almost equal number, technical and scale efficiency decreased. The greatest benefits were found whenever pre-merger efficiency scores were both low, suggesting that less efficient credit unions have the most to gain from merger, even if their partner is not more efficient, contrasting with the common view that gains should arise when assets are transferred from inefficient managers to efficient managers. In this study, the conclusion is drawn that mergers do not generate efficiency gains superior to those that non-merging credit unions can generate through internal growth. Ralston et al (2001) conclude that credit unions should focus on customer service along with efficiency if they are to continue to survive. While mergers may generate efficiency gains, they can reduce member satisfaction through reduction in staff or branch levels, or through problems caused when integrating systems, procedures and technologies (Rhoades, 1998). Finally, the study suggests that credit unions may best pursue the twin goals of efficiency and customer satisfaction by aligning themselves 'with other small financial institutions and centralised bodies to purchase aggregated services and to outsource specialised technology support and product innovation' (p 2302). The results of both the US and Australian studies are interesting and both highlight the problematic nature of mergers.

In keeping with the IE view on mergers, it is highly doubtful that a unitary perspective can be offered regarding the motivation and consequences of mergers. Therefore, rather than making any attempt to produce an all-embracing explanatory theory, we believe that it is best to let the case studies, at this stage, reveal the recurring issues and themes reported by our sample credit unions in terms of their experience of mergers. Our case studies reveal diverse patterns and unique circumstances. It is worth stressing that the participating credit unions were fully briefed that our remit was to consider credit union mergers that helped create credit unions that could better serve their communities.

The merger case studies: key themes

No single explanation could be found in the case studies regarding credit union merger activity. Rather, a wide range of themes emerged. Mergers were talked about in terms of combinations of factors, such as:

- a response to volunteer burnout;
- a response to regulatory burdens;
- to promote growth and attract new members;
- to achieve scale economies;
- to employ paid staff and engender greater professionalism;
- to offer wider services;
- to create a more financially viable credit union.

Our case study investigation of merger activity within the different credit unions allowed us to explore these various themes in some detail. One important recurring theme was that of crisis. Certainly in two case studies – namely, those involving Credit Unions E and G – there is clear evidence that merger activity had been triggered by financial crisis. Credit Union E, based in NI, has been involved in three mergers since 1999. All three mergers involved small community-based credit unions in close geographic proximity to Credit Union E. In two of the mergers, the underlying reason driving the merger process was insolvency in one credit union and financial irregularities in the second. The reason for the third merger, which occurred in 2001, lay in the simple fact that the credit union concerned "had simply run out of steam and they were done", and this was reflected in a non-functioning board.

Credit Union E found itself under intense pressure to "protect the good name of the movement" by intervening in the case of the two small, independent credit unions with financial difficulties. In one merger, the credit union taken on was insolvent. As the chair of Credit Union E relates:

> "We worked with them for about a year, by which stage so much money had haemorrhaged from their organisation that they couldn't pay their members. We took their members in good standing on and even though the share capital was only worth 20 pence in the pound, we gave the value of £1 for a £1 of share capital and made them full members of our credit union."

The second instance of merger driven by crisis involved Credit Union E rescuing a nearby credit union where there had been fraud. The net effect of these two mergers was to put Credit Union E into some short-term difficulties. For instance, the chair reported that "When the mergers took place this caused us real difficulty, in that our loan to share ratio was abysmal and has just recovered".

Credit Union E has always operated on the basis of employing paid staff and attributed the failings of the merged credit unions to an overreliance on the role of volunteers: "When you are operating out of a volunteer base and when you are just dithering around with a couple of wee manual ledgers you're never going to make it".

The chair pointed out that Credit Union E had overcome the difficulties engendered by the mergers and that the credit union had continued to grow and prosper. Interestingly, he was of the view that "It has been difficult financially, but, on balance, if I had the choice, I would do it all again".

Credit Union G, which is based in East London, has also been involved in three mergers. The first of these was in 1997 and involved a 200 member healthcare credit union. At that time, Credit Union G had a membership of 1,692 and an asset base of £1,746,223. The history of Credit Union G's merger activity can be usefully located in relation to the ever widening of their common bond, which occurred between 1996 and 1999. Initially, in 1996, Credit Union G moved from having a purely local authority employee common bond to a wider public sector common bond. Again, in 1999, the credit union then adopted a 'live or work' common bond. The nature of the common bond is a fundamental element governing the possibility of credit union mergers as the manager of Credit Union G highlights: "Even if there had been a crisis going on in credit unions, the regulator would not have allowed credit unions with uncommon bonds to merge".

The attraction for Credit Union G to widen its common bond is understandable given the growth of 'contracting out' within local authorities during the 1990s. It also served as a prerequisite in facilitating the first merger in 1997. Thus, as the manager of Credit Union G describes:

> "… with contracting out, suddenly a council-based credit union was in a position of having lots and lots of non-qualifying members overnight and therefore in breach of the law which has the limit of 10% non-qualifying members. The result of the new common bond being made all public sector employees therefore enabled this transfer to occur."

Equally, a second change of common bond occurred in 1999 when Credit Union G was the first employee-based credit union to change its common bond to a borough-wide 'live or work'. This has become a major trend in the UK since then, with local authority employee-based credit unions similarly opting for 'live or work' common bonds. This shift to wider 'live or work' common bonds has been coterminous with the philosophy of 'reaching out to the community' implicit in the financial inclusion agenda of many local authorities. The change of common bond by Credit Union G therefore provided a demonstration that others were to follow, and this has created a sea change in a trend towards wider common bonds. Up until then, the largest common bond encompassed the 100,000 population of the Isle of Wight. With its change to 'live or work', Credit Union G now had a potential membership of 250,000.

The second merger for Credit Union G involved a weak, struggling credit union nearby. As the manager put it, "… they couldn't manage things; they didn't have enough volunteers and had no paid staff".

The third merger, in 2001, gained national prominence and was widely reported in the press. Here, there had been alleged financial irregularities and the Financial Services Authority (FSA) had been called in by a whistleblower. The consequence of this was that, after conducting an audit, the FSA intended to liquidate the credit union concerned. A potential national crisis seemed possible:

> "Credit unions at that time did not have a share protection scheme in Britain, and if liquidation had occurred members would have lost real money which would have been immensely damaging for credit unions in the area, but also massively damaging for credit unions in Britain."

In these circumstances, Credit Union G felt it had no choice but to intervene and, to a large extent, was pressurised by the wider credit union movement to do so. However, the immediate consequence of this merger for Credit Union G was to weaken its own financial base, and it has taken until very recently to rebuild its capital base. The merger itself was only possible with the assistance of the wider credit union movement through donations to help make up some of the financial shortfall in the crisis credit union. Credit Union G has continued to grow and now has membership of some 4,800 and assets of £4.2 million. Much of this recent growth has been funded through grants aimed at supporting financial inclusion; Credit Union G received £65,000 in 2004 in grant support and £125,000 in 2005. In the view of the manager, the mergers have helped to attract new members, safeguarded members' savings and also created a more conducive environment in which services are provided. Credit Union G is nevertheless clear about the primary cause of the mergers: "In all three cases, the mergers were because of weak credit unions."

Credit Union G reported a changing role for volunteers where the credit union now employed staff to undertake operational tasks. The role of volunteers is still important on the board, and Credit Union G also sees a major role for volunteers "as vanguard soldiers in promoting credit unions in the community".

This promotional role is linked directly to the credit union's desire to tackle financial exclusion, where it has set itself the task of directly competing against doorstep lenders.

Credit Union C is the largest community-based credit union in Scotland, located in an industrial town that has lost most of its traditional heavy industry. In 2002, a smaller adjacent community credit union with 650 members and £480,000 assets merged with Credit Union C. This smaller credit union was 'a going concern' and was financially sound. Two main reasons were given for this merger. In the words of the full-time worker from the smaller credit union, the first reason was 'volunteer burnout':

"That was the main factor, that the board themselves started discussing it, they were all old, they had been doing it for 20 years, and, being honest, they were tired and there were no new ideas coming forward. That's why they started discussing the merger."

Similarly, this respondent indicated that increased regulation by the FSA had also been a major factor: "The FSA came into being and we were hit with all this bumf and we really couldn't cope with it".

The smaller credit union was stagnating, recognised this and saw the merger as the only opportunity available to them: "We knew that we were standing still and the only scope for growth was joining with [another credit union]".

The full-time worker in the smaller credit union helped drive the merger through. Although there was some dissension among members, the merger took place relatively smoothly and it was sold as a coming together of similar credit unions:

"It wasn't a takeover, and we were quick to point that out to our members. It was really a transfer of engagements."

It was reported that it is likely that the common bond of Credit Union C will, in the future, be further enlarged to encompass a wider geographical area, and this in turn might involve future mergers.

With Credit Union D, a change in their common bond from an 'employee' common bond to one that is based on a city-wide 'live or work', was the precursor to a series of nine mergers. These mergers or, more correctly, transfer of engagements, involved very small community credit unions within the city in which Credit Union D is located. The impetus for these mergers was the desire by Credit Union D to focus its future growth aspirations on the potential afforded by a city-wide common bond. However, the mergers have proved to be disappointing in heralding a new era of membership growth. As the manager of Credit Union D expresses it:

"… with hindsight we tried to do too much too soon. We were not a big credit union and we were expected to expand at the same time as transferring in eight other credit unions. I think we actually lost our core employee members … well, not lost them, but not gained them at the rate we were gaining them before, because we became too focused on promoting ourselves in the community, we sort of lost the plot in our core business."

It should be noted that Credit Union D received some grant funding to assist with the mergers, but now views the support received in a circumspect way:

"We've had some grant funding because of the mergers. I would say it's not done us too much good. As well as additional staffing costs, it was sought specifically for marketing and it was spent on advertising that hasn't actually increased our membership. The grant involved a lot of administration work and we did not receive as much as we had been promised. So my thoughts on grant funding aren't too positive and it's not something I'm going to go chasing after as the main substance of our business. Our aim is to regain our sustainability and budget accordingly."

Since the merger, the approach of Credit Union D has been to 'refocus' on their core membership and achieve clarity about their role. The manager of Credit Union D is dubious of 'grant chasing' and sees the role of the credit union as a financial institution providing value for money for its members:

"… I see us primarily as a financial company, not a social service, whereas I think a lot of credit unions see themselves the other way round. Recent research has shown that people don't join credit unions for ethical reasons. Promoting ourselves for our ethics is not particularly likely to increase our business, whereas we can retain our ethics and if we promote ourselves as a really good value for money financial services provider available to all then hopefully we will progress."

The dynamics of merger activity is qualitatively different in the case of Credit Union F in that it is the only merger that could be genuinely described as 'strategic'. This credit union is a large, employee-based credit union which had achieved a high level of membership penetration and was actively seeking ways in which it could expand its membership base. Although a number of credit unions with similar common bonds had met to discuss mergers, this came to nothing and Credit Union F decided to go for a national common bond to cover England and Wales. The intention behind this was to capture the membership of similar employee groups where credit union services did not exist. Other credit unions involved in the initial merger negotiations, however, did not appreciate this move, which contributed to the disintegration of merger talks: "Other [similar] credit unions saw the [national common bond] as a threat, but what we were interested in wasn't the 'territory' of these other credit unions but the [employee groups], which [have] no credit unions".

Credit Union F, which covered three separate employee groups in the north of England, targeted a similar credit union in the Midlands that covered some 21 employee groups throughout England and Wales. The rationale for the merger was mutual benefit: "The reason for the merger was that they wanted Version 2 status and we wanted to expand our membership base".

Credit Union F had attempted to grow its membership through expensive marketing campaigns but with little return, and this added to the impetus for merger. Additionally, even with a national common bond, the fact that employers will only recognise one credit union for payroll deductions created a powerful limiting factor in gaining membership within an employee group where a credit union already exists. Merging with another credit union therefore offered a better strategy for membership growth. Also, the merging credit union did have a small liquidity problem and this simply added to the case for merger.

Credit Union F sees itself as competing with the banks and building societies. Its loan to share ratio is approximately 100%. The merged credit union offers a competitive loan rate and special rates for new members. It uses capacity-based lending rather than a multiple of savings. It also pays a healthy dividend to members. The credit union's sound financial performance is, perhaps, a direct reflection of its membership base, where its members are in a job for life.

This merger was motivated purely by the pursuit of growth. As the credit union manager states: "It's a lot easier to grow through mergers, rather than trying to grow through increasing our own assets and building up our own reserves".

The merger has presented some new challenges for Credit Union F, especially in establishing a computer network between two offices one hundred miles apart. Merging a Version 2 and a Version 1 credit union similarly has posed challenges. However, the view is that the merger has been exceedingly successful and the manager of Credit Union F confidently predicts that it is only a matter of time before there will be one credit union serving all such employee groups in England and Wales.

As part of the case investigations, each credit union was asked to rank a predetermined list of merger 'drivers'. Table 6 provides summary details of the responses to this rating exercise. There are two areas that are identified as marginally more important reasons for merging than the rest. One is 'to create a financially viable credit union'. The average score for this criterion was 3.4 and three credit unions highlighted this reason as extremely important. In a related vein, the criterion 'to safeguard

Table 6: Summary of ranking exercise on merger drivers

Factors – 1 not important to 5 extremely important	C	D	E	F	G	Average score
To create a financially viable credit union	1	5	5	1	5	3.4
To safeguard members' savings	2	3	5	1	5	3.2
Difficulties due to the FSA's stricter regulatory regime	5	5	1	3	1	3.0
Widen and diversify common bond	3	5	1	4	1	2.8
Offer a wider range of services	2	5	1	4	1	2.6
Volunteer burnout	5	1	2	2	3	2.6
Avail of scale economies	1	5	1	5	1	2.6
Offer better priced services	1	5	1	2	1	2.0
Potential to move from 'volunteer-based' to 'paid staff-based'	3	3	1	1	1	1.8

members' savings' was also viewed as important, with an average score of 3.0 and with two credit unions identifying this reason as being extremely important.

Shared services as an alternative to mergers

An alternative to mergers is for credit unions to avail of 'shared services' in order to gain operational efficiencies and professionalism. Although well developed in other credit union systems, the UK has not seen this development take root until recently. As part of our investigations, a new shared services organisation which serves six credit unions in London was studied. This organisation is a company limited by guarantee and operates on a not-for-profit basis. It aims to provide services based on the sharing of resources such as computers, printers, staff, software and knowledge. Currently, it offers an accounting and membership management service, which includes maintaining the accounting and records database, and producing FSA returns and reports for credit union directors. This organisation was part grant-funded to help with initial start-up costs.

This organisation has ambitious plans to increase the number of credit unions it serves, and also to enhance the services it can provide. Thus, it aims to provide a members' enquiry service, including enquiries for loans, share withdrawals, the enrolment of new members and the issuing of members' statements. Similarly, it sees itself having a development role by helping credit union members to manage bad debt and deal with their member communications, and by undertaking research projects and funding bids on their behalf. The manager accepts that extending coverage within London is proving difficult and that his organisation is being squeezed: "We would love to be involved across London; the difficulty is that in a number of areas ABCUL is promoting this borough-wide common bond...".

Currently only serving small credit unions, the manager also recognised that, as these grew larger, his member credit unions might have an incentive to bring things back in-house: "It shouldn't take them too long to realise that instead of paying our fee they could pay a part-timer".

Although, to balance this, he pointed out that member credit unions were to a degree locked in due to their dependence on computing and technology services – for instance, the PayPoint system. His view was that shared services offered economies of scale and that they still had a long way to run before his client credit unions questioned the economic viability of shared services.

While shared services are a theoretical alternative to mergers, the reality is that, as an option, it is unavailable to the vast majority of credit unions, and the London case study shows that the provision of common services are very much in the infancy stage of development.

Final thoughts on mergers

The primary driver for mergers identified in most of the case studies is the existence of weak credit unions and the desire to create a financially viable credit union within which members' funds are safe. Beyond this, other factors interplay in unique ways to influence merger activity. As seen, the trend for wider common bonds is an important feature, which undoubtedly provides the necessary scope for mergers. In the majority of cases examined, the evidence was that mergers were often 'reactive', dealing with the problems encountered by small community credit unions. In this sense, these mergers were essentially 'mopping up' exercises. There was at least one instance where the merger involved more genuine 'strategic' reasons and here the merger was driven by growth aspirations. It is not accidental that this more strategic case involved a high performing credit union in Group 1. In some cases, the performance of the acquiring credit union was adversely affected by the merger, but this was recovered in the longer term. There was agreement in most of the case studies that, despite some of the problems encountered, the mergers had worked out. In assessing the case study mergers, it can be seen that each of them was unique and the product of particular circumstances, and this explains why the weighting of factors considered important by the credit unions involved differs in each case study.

5

Factors driving differential credit union performance

This aspect of the investigation is also case study in format. A total of 15 credit unions are considered. Seven of the credit unions are strong performers – that is, they have a Data envelopment analysis (DEA) score of 1 (see Table 4) and are categorised as a Group One credit union on the basis of the financial ratio analysis (see Table 3). Four credit unions are average-to-good performers – that is, they have a DEA score of between 0.5 and 0.75 and are classed as a Group Two credit union on the financial ratio analysis. Four credit unions are marginal performers with a DEA score between 0.3 and 0.5 and, from the financial ratios, are identified as Group Three credit unions. Group Four credit unions were not considered for case study. These credit unions are so weak that they will almost certainly not survive as they are presently constituted. Indeed, many of these credit unions are now in the process of amalgamating with other 'stronger' credit unions.

The 15 credit unions under case investigation were geographically spread: five in Scotland, four in England and Wales and six in Northern Ireland (NI). Four of these credit unions could be considered rural credit unions, with the remainder urban. There was also a mix of common bond types: six community or residential, four 'live or work', two employment or industrial and three associational. In terms of affiliation to trade bodies, seven were affiliated to the Association of British Credit Unions (ABCUL), five were affiliated to the Irish League of Credit Unions (ILCU), two to the Scottish League of Credit Unions (SLCU) and one to the Ulster Federation of Credit Unions (UFCU). Finally, there was considerable variation in the size distribution of the credit unions, with the smallest having an asset base of approximately £280,000 and the largest having assets of approximately £40 million.

The case studies took place at the premises of the credit union in question and, in most cases, were carried out with a mix of the office manager, the treasurer and the chair of the credit union board. To encourage interviewees to be as open as possible, it was stated that the interviews would be reported in such a way as to prevent specific statements being attributed to particular individuals or associated with individual credit unions.

The objective of this part of the analysis is to undertake a compare and contrast investigation of credit unions in an effort to identify operational aspects which may contribute to the relative success of individual credit unions. Information on the operational aspects of the 15 case study credit unions is presented in Tables 7, 8 and 9. The data are categorised in terms of the three groups (One, Two and Three). Where financial information is presented, it is for year end 2003. In a more negative vein, this compare and contrast methodology will also be utilised to consider those aspects of a credit union's operations which hinder development. This, however, should not be taken to mean that a unique template exists which, if implemented, will in every case succeed in transforming a poorly performing credit union into a strong performer. Indeed, what might work and be appropriate for one credit union may not be appropriate for another, perhaps because of differences in credit union ethos and philosophy. Furthermore, it should not be taken that, because a credit union is identified as a strong performing, Group One credit union, all aspects of its business model are performing as they should. The ensuing discussion will highlight aspects where improvements could be made by *all* credit unions.

Two strong but different credit unions

Before we embark on our investigation of the operational aspects contributing to the success or failure of individual credit unions, let us consider two quite different credit unions, both of which have been identified as strong performing Group One credit unions. The reason for considering these two credit unions is to emphasise the point that an off-the-shelf success template for all credit unions is not achievable. The two credit unions are identified in Table 7 as Credit Union I and Credit Union M. Both are affiliated to the same trade association, both came into existence in the 1960s and both have a common bond identified as 'community or residential'. This is where the similarity ends. Credit Union I viewed its primary function as that of a financial cooperative providing its members with financial services for the maximum benefit of its members regardless of the level of profit generated and the amount of dividends paid on members' savings. Credit Union I also saw the purpose of the board as making policy. Staff were hired, directed by a manager and did all the work. Credit Union I is a full service financial provider, it has a city-wide common bond and a broad socioeconomic mix of members, who are served by 8 full-time and 16 part-time staff (see Table 8). Compare this profile to that of Credit Union M, which viewed its primary function as that of providing services for the financially excluded who would otherwise be unable to access credit. The board of directors of Credit Union M saw themselves as a group of like-minded people taking responsibility for defining and supporting the credit union philosophy. Consensus decision-making was a key characteristic, with the board working together on governance, management and day-to-day operations. Credit Union M provides only a basic savings and loans service (in 2004 it offered a dividend of 3% and the loan rate was 12.68 APR, although there was an interest loan rebate of 30%). Members of the credit union are drawn from an area of social disadvantage, with Credit Union M unable to expand its common bond because of the proximity of other credit unions. There are three part-time staff (total annual wage bill of £8,000) with board members heavily involved in front-office operations (see Table 8).

Both Credit Union I and Credit Union M are a success with robust financial ratios (see Table 7). Their operational structures are, however, very different, as indeed are their philosophies as to the role and modus operandi of a credit union. It is these stark differences which complicate any relative assessment of the factors behind a credit union's success.

The importance of benchmark data

Most of the information, based on 2003 financial data, detailed in Table 7 is similar to that in Table 3 (first nine pieces of information). Also provided in Table 7, but not Table 3, is information on the asset size, age, bond type, region of origin and trade association of the respective credit unions. The 2003 data on individual credit unions portrays the seven Group One credit unions as larger, more operationally efficient and offering a better return to members than credit unions in Groups Two and Three. For example, the ratio operating expenses as a percentage of operating income highlights that all the credit unions in Group One, perhaps with the exception of one, are efficiently run organisations. (The ILCU has a target for this ratio of less than 43% as part of its PEARLS recommended ratios, although it also emphasises that a lower target for this ratio may be manageable in larger credit unions because of economics of scale.) Only Credit Union K in Group One has a relatively high operating expense to operating income ratio. Credit Union K has, in recent times, amalgamated with a number of smaller credit unions but has kept collection points where the smaller credit unions previously existed. This has probably forced up the operating costs of Credit Union K to a level that is unlikely to be sustainable longer term. (Increased operating costs and reduced dividend payments were also noted in Chapter Four as short-term consequences in the case investigations of merging credit unions.)

Examination of operating expenses as a percentage of operating income for Group Two credit unions reveals that each of the four credit unions exceeds the target of 43%. In the case of Group Three credit unions, this ratio is much higher again and, indeed, raises questions as to the ability of certain credit unions (for example, Credit Union V) to sustain its current level of operational capacity.

The ratio 'return as a percentage of average member funds' is a measure of the financial benefit of the credit union to its members. The figures reported in Table 7 highlight that accrued benefits are greater for Group One credit unions. For two of the Group Three credit unions, the documented figure is 0%, which indicates that these credit unions neither provided a dividend nor a loan interest rebate to members.

The capital adequacy ratio also highlights a fundamental difference between credit unions in the respective groups. In this instance, all credit unions in Groups One and Two have adequate levels of capital. This is not the case for those credit unions in Group Three, where reserves trend around 5%.

In this brief analysis of the information detailed in Table 7, we have chosen to emphasise three ratios which were used to present a picture of broadly uniform differences between Group One, Group Two and Group Three credit unions. More generally, however, this discussion should highlight the importance of individual credit unions being able to benchmark all aspects of their operation against comparable credit unions. PEARLS is one such vehicle through which a comparable analysis can be undertaken. PEARLS has been used by the Irish League of Credit Unions (ILCU) since 2002, while the Association of British Credit Unions (ABCUL) has piloted a PEARLS project with 20 credit unions and hopes to roll out the programme to others.

More generally, the provision of appropriate benchmark data to all UK credit unions may help individual credit unions identify aspects of their business which require action. Let us end this aspect of the case investigation by highlighting the potential benefits which may result from the use of benchmark data. The treasurer of Credit Union R argued that PEARLS had been instrumental in identifying above average expenditure levels by Credit Union R, which now has policies in place to help rectify overexpenditure: "What it is turning out is, in fact, good, straight statistics to work on".

Premises and staff

In Table 8, information is presented on the credit unions' business premises. The material detailed includes opening times, whether the credit union has collection points, how the premises are financed and the interviewers' perceptions of the quality of the premises. In Table 8, information has also been collated on staffing and includes whether an office manager is in place, the mix of full- and part-time staff, whether the credit union relies on volunteers to run back- and front-office operations, and the interviewers' general impressions of the credit union's staff/volunteers.

Centrally situated high-profile, good quality, member-financed premises owned in full by the credit union with convenient opening hours operated primarily by a mix of full-time and part-time staff reporting to a full-time manager appears to be a common denominator across credit unions identified as Group One (Credit Union M is the one exception; as indicated earlier, it has quite restrictive opening hours and relies heavily on volunteers to fulfil all functions). This contrasts with credit unions in Group Three. In this group, the credit union's place of business is invariably basic and spartan. The credit union does not have outright ownership of its premises or, if it does, this will have been achieved through grant income rather than member funds. The credit union usually relies heavily on volunteers for back- and front-office processing and, in those cases where credit unions are able to make full- or part-time appointments, this will, again, have been achieved by way of grant income instead of member funds. Finally, opening hours tend to be limited and usually restricted to three or four days in the week.

In this comparison of staff and premises between the three groups, a number of issues immediately come to the fore. The first and most obvious is that, on average, credit unions in Groups Two and Three are much smaller in terms of assets and members than those in Group One, and their scale of operations may not as yet justify the investment of member funds in premises and full-time staff. Having made this point, in our discussions with credit unions in Group One, the importance that they place on having good quality premises staffed by full-time employees in growing their credit union did become obvious. Credit Union H, for example, moved into new premises in May 1998, at which stage its assets were of the order of £1 million; six years later, in September 2004, the asset base of Credit Union H stood at £8 million. While increases for other credit unions were not as dramatic as in the case of Credit Union H, the opening of new premises was invariably associated with a sustained, cumulative upswing in membership, paralleled by a similar stepwise increase in total assets. Credit Union J, now conducting business from recently constructed, self-financed, high-specification premises, where previously a portacabin was used, suggested that the new premises would broaden the membership appeal of the credit union by helping to shake the tag of it 'as the poor man's financial institution'. While there may be some credence in new premises helping to widen the appeal, not just of Credit Union J, but of all credit unions, also important in

Table 7(1): Financial data 2003, Group One credit unions

Group One	H	I	J	K	L	M	N
Members	4,000	15,000	5,000	12,500	6,210	1,800	9,340
Member change	5.6	1.0	4.2	11.0	3.2	1.1	11.7
Shares+ savings/ member	£1,612	£2,403	£800	£900	£1,382	£1,896	£793
Loans/shares	91.8	61.0	85.0	104.0	95.8	99.21	104.7
Operating expenditure/ operating income	25.87	26.2	23.6	50.0	35.06	40.01	55.46
Loan provisions/ average loans	1.25	2.47	0.79	0.39	0.1	1.0	0.4
Net interest received/ average loans	8.93	10.93	10.61	11.03	9.53	8.76	11.0
Return/average members' funds	4.61	6.01	7.05	4.79	4.17	5.44	4.8
Capital/assets	16.84	10.71	12.83	9.92	11.55	10.88	7.92
Asset size	£8 m	£38 m	£4 m	£12 m	£10 m	£4 m	£8 m
Age	40	41	27	17	15	37	25
Bond type	Live/work	Community	Community	Live/work	Emp/Ind	Community	Association
Region of origin	NI	NI	Scotland	England/Wales	Scotland	NI	England/Wales
Trade association	ILCU	ILCU	SLCU	ABCUL	ABCUL	ILCU	ABCUL

Table 7(2): Financial data 2003, Groups Two and Three credit unions

Groups Two/Three	O	P	Q	R	S	T	U	V
Members	1,090	1,700	1,500	2,500	1,400	1,200	2,400	2,500
Member change	7.0	1.0	0.3	0.5	–2.0	3.0	1.0	1.5
Shares/member	£972	£1,663	£1,924	£1,093	£550	£199	£934	£467
Loans/shares	106.0	97.13	52.3	42.0	83.0	126.0	87.12	71.8
Operating expenditure/operating income	99.87	47.74	49.63	55.32	59.0	94.33	70.26	164.8
Loan provisions/average loans	0.8	1.24	0.6	0.98	10.18	2.47	0.3	1.86
Net interest received/average loans	11.08	10.68	11.35	12.56	9.3	11.33	10.84	11.61
Return/average members' funds	0.05	5.0	2.5	2.0	0.0	0.0	1.0	1.0
Capital/assets	13.22	11.18	10.19	10.23	4.5	5.8	4.4	5.6
Asset size	£1.3 m	£3.1 m	£3.2 m	£3 m	£550,000	£280,000	£2.4 m	£1.3 m
Age	24	26	37	38	14	7	19	34
Bond type	Association	Association	Community	Live/work	Community	Community	Emp/Ind	Live/work
Region of origin	Scotland	England/Wales	Northern Ireland	Northern Ireland	Northern Ireland	Scotland	England/Wales	England/Wales
Trade association	ABCUL	ABCUL	ILCU	ILCU	UFCU	SLCU	ABCUL	ABCUL

the upswing in membership was that new premises invariably come hand-in-hand with longer and more 'traditional' opening hours, plus a commensurate increase in staff. In addition, the interviewers noted that credit unions with their own purpose-built premises were better able to create a physical demarcation between front- and back-office functions. Front offices, particularly in the case of credit unions in Group One, were then used to promote the credit union and its services to existing and potential members. For example, as part of its front office, Credit Union H had a play area for children, while Credit Union I had a series of commissioned artwork highlighting the benefits of being a credit union member. Also, all credit unions in Group One had material on display advertising the products and services that they offer.

It is also worth noting that a high-profile front office is more important for community credit unions than for either associational or employer-based credit unions. In the case of association and employer based-credit unions, direct payroll deduction is often used in repaying loans and mitigates the necessity of transacting business by 'dropping in' to the front office. Credit Union O has a common bond of association, with members of that association being self-employed. Innovatively, Credit Union O has used the 8,000 strong network of PayPoint machines as a vehicle through which members may repay loans. The office manager of Credit Union O commented that "The use of the

Table 8(1): Staff and premises, Group One credit unions

Group One	H	I	J	K	L	M	N
Staff (full time)	4	8	1	18	8	0	2
Staff (part time)	1	16	0	7	1	3	0
Manager	Yes	Yes	Yes	Yes	Yes	No	Yes
Volunteers (front/back office)	No	No	Yes	No	No	Yes	No
Staff/ volunteers (general impression)	Excellent	Excellent	Good	Good	Good	Good	Average
Own premises	Yes	Yes	Yes	Yes	Yes	Yes	Yes
Premises grant-financed	No	No	No	No	No	No	No
Days open in week	6	5	5	5	5	3	5
Other collection points	Yes	No	Yes	Yes	No	No	No
Premises (impression)	Excellent	Excellent	Excellent	Good	Good	Excellent	Average
Premises (location)	Excellent	Excellent	Excellent	Excellent	Good	Excellent	Good

Table 8(2): Staff and premises, Groups Two and Three and credit unions

Groups Two/Three	O	P	Q	R	S	T	U	V
Staff (full time)	2	3	2	0	0	0	3*	5*
Staff (part time)	2	1	4	4	0	1	3	1
Manager (full time)	Yes	Yes	Yes	No	No	No	Yes	Yes
Volunteers (front/ back office)	No	No	Yes	Yes	Yes	Yes	Yes	Yes
Staff volunteers (general impression)	Excellent	Good	Good	Excellent	Good	Good	Good	Good
Own premises	Yes	Yes	Yes	Yes	Yes	No	Yes	Yes
Premises grant-financed	No	No	No	No	Yes	–	No	Yes
Days open in week	5	5	4	4	3	3	4	4
Other collection points	No	No	No	No	Yes	No	No	Yes
Premises (impression)	Average	Good	Good	Excellent	Good	Poor	Excellent	Average
Premises (location)	Average	Good	Good	Excellent	Good	Good	Excellent	Poor

Note: *Staff in part financed from grants or salary subsidisation.

network of PayPoint machines has reduced the volume of business transacted directly through the office by about 40%".

Irrespective of credit union bond type, acquiring bespoke and staffed premises is a goal of most credit unions. If one considers credit unions in Group One, it is also clear that these credit unions have not entered into such expansionary plans until they were in a position to finance such developments from the retained funds of members. These credit unions epitomise the 'self-help' principles on which the credit union movement is forged. These credit unions, for the most part, have not availed (or been able to avail) of outside grants to fast track staff appointments and the construction of premises. While this probably has meant that the pace of development of the credit union has been slower than it might otherwise have been, it also means that the credit union has resilience and the capability of withstanding the pressures of today's financial environment without outside assistance. This situation is in contrast to the two new start, 'fast growth' credit unions case studied in Chapter Three. These two credit unions have, to some extent, supplanted the 'self-help' principle through availing of outside support, and now have in place operational structures which at present are inconsistent with the level of member business being conducted. As emphasised in Chapter Three, these credit unions must significantly grow their asset base if they are to continue in business when (and if) their financial safety net ends.

Again, through the present case studies, we can juxtapose the situation of a credit union helped by grants but now in a position where, if grants do not continue, service levels may need to be reduced, with a credit union which has developed at its own pace and is comfortable with its current service provision levels. The credit unions in question are Credit Union H, which is a Group One, strong performing credit union, and Credit Union V, which is a Group Three, marginal performing credit union.

Consider first of all Credit Union H. It has a 'live or work' common bond, has now £8 million in assets and over 4,000 members, and is in robust financial health. The history of Credit Union H is one of financial rectitude, only entertaining new initiatives, be they acquisition of new premises, the appointment of staff or indeed the implementation of an IT strategy, if they could be financed from retained earnings. Credit Union H was established in 1964. It first appointed a part-time worker in 1970, at a wage of £3. A second worker, again part time, was appointed in 1983. Today, the credit union has four full-time and two part-time staff. For the first 15 years, the credit union only opened on a Friday night; opening hours were extended to a Saturday in 1979 and then also to a Tuesday in 1981. Today, the credit union is open six days a week. The credit union purchased an old building in 1979 (cost £6,700). This building was demolished and a new credit union office constructed and officially opened in 1981. It is interesting to note from the credit union's own records the problems faced by Credit Union H at that time, but also the emphasis placed on 'self-help':

> "At one stage it was suggested that the premises should be sold again ... eventually agreement was reached that there could be a credit union provided savings were increased by the amount needed to do the work. This involved going out into the highways and byways to find people who had surplus money which they could invest for at least two years in the credit union."

The pace of expansion by Credit Union H necessitated that even larger premises were required and were purchased in 1986 for £57,000. Renovation and refurbishment was not started until 1997, with the offices officially opened in May 1998 (total contract cost, £248,000). Credit Union H's most recent sizeable investment was in 2004, when £45,000 was spent on a complete new computer system to service both its main and subsidiary office. Again, the source of financing was that of retained earnings.

Credit Union V has a 'live or work' common bond and now has £1.3 million in assets and 2,500 qualifying members. It was established in 1970 and, primarily because the credit union served an area of significant social disadvantage, it has been able to avail of grants to support premises, staff and equipment. Credit Union V has its own premises and at present five full-time staff and one part-time staff member. In 2003, almost 50% of its total income came from grants, with grant income almost twice that of interest income from members' loans. Credit Union V estimates that two of the full-time and the only part-time staff member are supported through grant income. The income support for staff comes from the local social inclusion partnership. It is up for renewal in 2006, and Credit Union V states that without the renewal of these grants it will be difficult to maintain staffing at current levels. In a general comment on the impact of grants, Credit Union V stated:

> "The biggest effect that it has had on this credit union is that it has made us accustomed to live in a lifestyle that we cannot necessarily afford ... if it had been a normal growth some of the decisions that had been taken wouldn't have been taken as easily. For example, we are sitting with 12 PCs here so that there is one in every room and we got all of these through grant money but the running costs, the maintenance costs, we don't as easily take into the picture. So I think capital funding has a bit of a backlash in that you are in a kind of false operating situation."

The false situation which Credit Union V finds itself in can be emphasised by simply comparing its level of staffing with that of Credit Union H. The latter has four full-time and two part-time staff and services 4000 members, with the assets of the credit union now £8 million. Credit Union V, as indicated, has £1.3 million in assets, 2,500 members and five full-time and one part-time staff members.

The creation of a dependency culture as a consequence is clearly an issue which has exercised Credit Union V, with the interviewee adding the following measured comments:

> "I wouldn't ever say that there shouldn't be grants. For us the ideal would be that we wouldn't get grants for offering core services. They would very much have to stand on their own. But if we were undertaking specific work, like for financial inclusion when we predicted that any income generated from that would never be enough to meet the overheads, then that's the kind of thing that I think should be grant funded ... because we are meeting a social agenda rather than, say, a business agenda with those."

Volunteers

As highlighted in Table 8, most of the credit unions in the case investigations employ staff. A comparison of the three groups suggests that, as we move from Group Three through to Group One, this is increasingly at the expense of volunteer use. Indeed, only Credit Union J and Credit Union M in Group One use volunteers to help perform the day-to-day functions of the credit union. The general view expressed by interviewees representing credit unions in Group One was that, given the scale of their operations and the sophistication of their business, the use of volunteers might hamper the good functioning of the credit union. While such sentiments may be understandable, they are regrettable in that using and training volunteers contributes to the creation of social capital in the area in which the credit union is based. Of course, for most Group Three credit unions, the day-to-day good function of the credit union would not happen without volunteers. Consider Credit Union S, which has £550,000 in assets and primarily services a socially disadvantaged community. Credit Union S has a main office, open three days per week, plus three other collection points, each open one day per week for restricted hours. Twelve volunteers, none of whom is a board member, run the office and collection points. Credit Union S also indicated it is this network of volunteers from which board members are 'groomed'.

A credit union's stage of development therefore appears to influence whether volunteers are used in a significant way in the day-to-day running of the credit union. This, however, is not a hard and fast rule. We have also seen that the philosophy and ethos of the credit union will influence the extent to which volunteers are used. The earlier case history of Credit Union M, a Group One credit union, describes a credit union that has never lost the pure philosophy of credit unionism and remains true to its volunteer roots. In contrast, Credit Union V, a Group Three credit union, is less comfortable with the contribution which can be made by some volunteers and suggests that certain volunteers add to a credit union's workload: "We can only really have people in as volunteers if they contribute. We cannot really afford to be a training agency to support people out of the community or helping them into work."

The board of directors

The need for greater member involvement

At this juncture, let us now move on to consider another group of unpaid volunteers – that is, the board of directors of the credit union. Leighton and Thain (1997) state that the selection of directors is one of the critical factors in determining how effectively a corporation is governed. Information on board structure, the skill sets of directors, the planning activities of the board and the extent and type of training available to new directors is detailed in Table 9. In this part of the analysis, let us first consider the initial six pieces of information in Table 9 – the number of directors on the board, their average age, the average length of time spent on the board, whether, at the most recent AGM, there were more candidates for election than board vacancies, the attendance at the AGM, and whether the credit union uses a nominating committee. Perhaps the most surprising finding is that each of the 15 credit unions had at their most recent AGM the same number of candidates for election as there were vacancies. In essence, this is tantamount to the membership of these credit unions having no real choice in the selection of directors. This lack of choice is further compounded when the average length of service of directors is considered. In Table 9, the average period stretches from 5 years (Credit Union V) to 18 years (Credit Union R), with the norm about 10 years. In the UK, each director is required to stand for re-election every 3 years, and the general practice among all credit unions is that one third of the board stands for election each year. This requirement, in conjunction with the norm of around 10 years' service by directors, implies that directors are running for re-election unopposed time and time again. The unopposed nature of this process suggests that incumbent directors may not be required to defend, or even present, their past record as a director of the credit union, which may be unhelpful to the good functioning of the credit union.

Also detailed in Table 9 is the number of directors on each of the boards, and this number varies between 7 and 15. The minimum number of directors of credit union boards is established by legislation; however, within this stricture, trade associations may place numerical requirements on directors. For ABCUL affiliates, the required number of directors is not less than 5; for ILCU, 5-15; for UFCU, not less than 12 nor more than 21; and for SFCU not less than 5. From Table 9, it appears that Group One credit unions have, in general, greater numbers of directors than either Group Two or Group Three credit unions. This may suggest that there are more demands on larger credit unions, thus requiring larger boards to share the workload. Whether this is the case or not, it is interesting to note the following comment from the manager of Credit Union O, who argued that his board size of seven was too small and was hindering the operation of the credit union:

> "I find huge difficulty in having the smaller board, as the board includes the credit committee as well. This means that three members leave board meetings halfway through to discuss credit committee business, at many meetings someone else needs to leave early, leaving just three directors at the end of the meeting. If a big decision needs to be made, this is often postponed until the next meeting. (The reason for this is practical rather that technical as, if a quorum is present at the start of a meeting, the meeting remains quorate even if four directors have left.) This impacts on my ability to do my job properly."

The question then arises as to why certain credit unions may have a suboptimal size of credit union board and/or an almost continual recycling of existing directors. The answer appears to be member apathy. A recurring theme in the case studies was the difficulty the credit union faced in attracting members to serve on the credit union board, although it should be noted that only 5 of the 15 credit unions in the case analysis indicated that they operated a nominating committee. Four of these five credit unions were affiliated to the ILCU, which requires the appointment of a nominating committee (ILCU Standard Rules for Credit Unions Rule 73). The following comments from Credit Union K, which has 12,000 members, were typical: "We have 13 board members and we are supposed to have three supervisors; that's 16 people. You try finding 16 competent people willing to give up all that time. It's tough."

While in a similar vein, Credit Union O stated:

> "There are seven directors in the credit union. The credit union has huge difficulty in getting directors ... We hope to bring in four or five new directors at the next AGM. They will be the first new influx in four years."

More generally, the merger case studies in Chapter Four revealed that two of the main drivers in small credit unions transferring engagements into larger credit unions were volunteer burnout and difficulty in attracting volunteers. Furthermore, the 'new' credit union created as a consequence of the merger considered that its larger scale might help in attracting volunteers.

Member apathy can also be seen in AGM attendance. The reported figures in Table 9 are inclusive of directors and credit union management and highlight, especially for Group Two and Group Three credit unions, limited member interest in the governance of their credit union.

Skill sets of credit union directors

Branch and Baker (1998) state that 'the ability of directors to ... monitor or control [a credit union] depends upon their business acumen and management skills' (p 1). The authors additionally add that the demands placed on directors in terms of financial and business expertise increase with the size and sophistication of the credit union. The World Council of Credit Unions (WOCCU) (2002) has itself detailed optimal requirements for credit union directors:

> Each board member must be a member of the credit union and capable of the following so that they are an active and effective part of the board: ability to read and interpret financial statements; basic understanding of the laws governing the credit union; knowledge of risk measurement and effective management; knowledge of and a commitment to credit union philosophy; familiarity with asset/liability management; familiarity with lending and collections; familiarity with marketing concepts; ability to work as part of a team; ability to commit enough time to successfully complete all of the job duties and responsibilities; and strong oral communication skills. (p 1)

In Table 9, information is detailed on the percentages of boards of directors that meet a selection of the WOCCU (2002) 'job prerequisites'. Systematic differences do not emerge across the three credit union groups, and the general impression gained is that many credit union boards do not have the full complement of requisite skills to fulfil the requisite roles and functions of the credit union governance process. For example, Table 9 highlights that many boards have almost no directors with a 'knowledge of risk management and effective management', 'familiarity with asset liability management' or 'familiarity with marketing concepts'. Perhaps more worryingly, many boards have a considerable number of directors with no 'ability to read and interpret financial statements'. This contrasts with the fact that each case investigation indicated that all their board members had 'knowledge of and a commitment to credit union philosophy'. Reflecting generally on credit union

Table 9(1): The credit union board, Group One credit unions

Group One	H	I	J	K	L	M	N
Number of directors	15	11	7	13	8	9	12
Average age	56	67	63	58	45	54	45
Average period on board	9	15	10	10	8	17	9
Board vacancies/applications	Same	Same	Same	Same	Same	Same	Same
Attendance at last AGM	150	280	100	125	18	19	130
Nominating committee	NO	YES	NO	YES	NO	YES	NO
Board skills							
Read and interpret financial statements (%)	50	50	100	25	100	100	50
Knowledge of risk management (%)	50	50	50	50	100	50	50
Knowledge of credit union philosophy (%)	100	100	100	100	100	100	100
Knowledge of asset liability management (%)	25	25	0	25	0	25	50
Familiarity with marketing (%)	25	50	0	25	0	25	25
Ability to work as a team (%)	75	100	100	100	100	100	100
Planning activities							
Long-term strategic plan	YES	NO	YES	YES	YES	NO	NO
1-year operating plan	YES	YES	YES	YES	YES	YES	NO
1-year operating budget	YES	YES	NO	YES	YES	NO	YES
Target and objective setting for CU	YES	YES	NO	YES	YES	YES	YES
Formal training for new directors	NO	NO	YES	NO	NO	NO	YES
Reading material	NO	YES	NO	NO	YES	NO	NO
Internal articulation	NO	YES	NO	NO	NO	NO	NO
External training seminars	NO	YES	YES	NO	NO	NO	YES

boards, which probably had skill sets similar to those detailed in our case investigations, Branch and Baker (1998, p 2) noted that credit union boards can 'be very responsive to local social issues but fail to manage the financial business aspects that become increasingly complex as the credit union grows'.

While not typical of the credit unions in our case investigations, Credit Union P, when asked if directors with specific skills were sought when new appointments were made to the board, replied:

> "Just somebody with a bit of common sense, that's all you need, you just need common sense."

This same credit union, when asked about the challenges faced over the near future, replied:

> "Unfortunately loans have been dropping and that is due to membership dropping, a lot of the guys are retiring from the trade so what we need to do is get the young guys in, because you can't have your membership dropping, 25 years on and you have lost nearly a thousand members."

For Credit Union P, with its declining membership, to have an individual or individuals with marketing expertise on the board might well be useful in helping to formulate a strategy to boost membership.

Table 9(2): The credit union board, Groups Two and Three credit unions

Groups Two/Three	O	P	Q	R	S	T	U	V
Number of directors	7	7	7	13	12	12	10	7
Average age	54	55	49	63	49	65	55	60
Average period on board	8	7	10	18	10	6	6	5
Board vacancies/applications	Same	Same	Same	Same	Same	Same	Same	Same
Attendance at last AGM	18	50	119	22	12	17	26	40
Nominating committee	NO	NO	YES	YES	NO	NO	NO	NO
Board skills								
Read and interpret financial statements (%)	25	25	75	25	25	25	25	25
Knowledge of risk management (%)	25	25	75	75	25	25	25	25
Knowledge of credit union philosophy (%)	75	100	75	75	75	75	75	75
Knowledge of asset liability management (%)	0	25	50	25	25	25	25	25
Familiarity with marketing (%)	25	25	75	50	0	25	25	0
Ability to work as a team (%)	50	75	100	100	100	25	75	50
Planning activities								
Long-term strategic plan	NO	YES	NO	NO	NO	YES	NO	NO
1-year operating plan	YES	YES	NO	NO	NO	YES	YES	YES
1-year operating budget	NO	NO	NO	NO	NO	NO	YES	NO
Target and objective setting for CU	YES	YES	YES	NO	NO	NO	YES	NO
Formal training for new directors	YES	YES	NO	NO	NO	YES	YES	NO
Reading material	NO	NO	NO	NO	YES	NO	YES	NO
Internal articulation	NO	NO	NO	NO	NO	YES	NO	NO
External training seminars	YES	YES	NO	NO	NO	NO	NO	NO

Another example of the importance of having a breadth of skills on the board can be seen in recent problems faced by Credit Union K. In this instance, the problems centred on a breakdown in working relations between management and a member of the supervisory committee, which culminated in the manager refusing to attend board meetings. When Credit Union K was asked to comment on whether the credit union sought directors with specific skills, the reply was "We are looking for somebody that has the right sort of skills, and that is not necessarily qualifications, but has experience, life skills, but also the commitment to the credit union".

Again, the interviewers were left with the impression that, if the board of Credit Union K had had access to personnel skills, it may have been able to cope more easily with the aforementioned breakdown in working relationships.

While these two examples are useful in highlighting the importance of a board of directors having a breadth of appropriate skills, this point can be made more generally by an examination of the strategic and planning activities carried out by the credit union. Table 9 provides information on whether the credit unions in the case analysis undertake certain strategic and planning activities. Credit unions were asked whether they had: a long-term strategic plan; an operating plan with credit union goals and objectives for the upcoming year; an annual operating budget against which monthly activities are measured; and whether they set annual targets and objectives for the credit union. Each of these four activities could be viewed as good practice for the credit union, with some of the activities being specifically encouraged by the FSA.

Looking across the three groups of credit unions, there again does not appear to be any real pattern, with credit unions in each of the groups indicating that they undertake some or all of these activities. (It should be emphasised that no assessment of the actual quality of the planning procedures was carried out by the interviewers for those credit unions indicating that they had such procedures in place.) Having made the point that many credit unions have these planning documents in place, that still leaves a number which do not. For example, Credit Union I, which has an asset base of £38 million, does not "develop and document a long term strategic plan with credit union goals and objectives for more than one year ahead", while a typical comment when expanding on the use or otherwise of planning documents came from the manager of Credit Union O:

> "The credit union does not document and develop long-term strategic plans, though
> we intend to do so. We do have a business plan that I made, that focuses over five years,
> but that was only as a response to an FSA request, so it was more of a solution to an
> immediate problem than a long-term document."

It is also noticeable from Table 9 that a sizeable number, particularly credit unions in Groups Two and Three, do not develop an annual operating budget against which monthly activities are measured. A procedure such as this is good practice and the failure of credit unions to have it in place is likely to hamper development.

Where such planning and strategic documents are missing, the problem lies with the board of directors. Although not specifically commenting on credit unions, the Combined Code (2003, p 4) stated that 'The board should set the company's strategic aims, ensuring that the necessary financial and human resources are in place for the company to meet its objectives and review management performance'.

Again, the failure of such documents to be in place may be due to the board lacking the requisite skill sets to at least recognise the importance of such planning documents, if not actually to create these documents themselves.

The specific and the more general examples have been used to highlight the importance of having a varied skills set on the credit union board. In practical terms, this may be difficult to achieve. For organisations other than credit unions, the potential for suitable candidates is only limited by the area of search established by the searchers. For credit unions, directors must be drawn from the membership, which may, for certain credit unions, hamper their ability to create a board of directors that possess the attributes, qualifications and experience necessary to fulfil the roles and functions of the credit union governance process.

Director training

The academic literature stresses that the qualifications of directors, individually as well as collectively as a board, is a vital component in the board's ability to fulfil its advisory, oversight and leadership functions and responsibilities[6]. In that the 'pool of expertise' from which directors are drawn is restricted by virtue of the credit union's common bond, the training of directors has enhanced

---

[6] The Centre for Research into Socially Inclusive Services (CRSIS) at Heriot-Watt University was commissioned by the Scottish Executive to audit training provision and training needs for credit union volunteers in Scotland, to develop a toolkit for credit unions to undertake skills audits for their volunteer workforces, and to make recommendations regarding appropriate training delivery mechanisms (see Chapman et al, 2004).

importance. The credit unions in the case investigation were asked whether they had a formal training programme for all new directors and, if so, what format the programme followed.

From Table 9, it can be seen that six credit unions state that they offer a formal training programme for new directors. Surprisingly, a large number (nine) do not, including some of those credit unions categorised as belonging to Group One. When, however, the interviewers probed into the type and quality of training provided, it materialised that there was little difference between those credit unions which intimated that they had formal procedures and those which indicated they had not.

For example, Credit Union I, which stated that it did not have formal training for new directors, added: "Although there is no formal training plans at present, we do carry out in-house induction and notify directors of all ILCU training courses. Directors also have access to materials supplied by the ILCU".

Credit Union I also adopted the practice of 'potential' directors shadowing existing directors for a period of one year prior to standing for election to the board.

Credit Union P argued that it had a formal training programme but, when questioned further, revealed that training consisted of attending workshops at the trade association's AGM: "Four out of the seven directors on the board have been on training at the weekend conference up at Blackpool – the workshops".

The general impression gained by the interviewers was that all credit unions undertook training of some form. For some credit unions, the level of training was very restricted. This was particularly true of credit unions which had a very limited turnover of directors, which, in Table 9, can be discerned from the average length of time members have served on the board. It was also true of credit unions such as M in Table 8, where the credit union board assumed all the functions of the organisation – governance, management and operations – and consequently had an in-depth knowledge of the credit union which they could impart to new directors. For the other credit unions, while much more training was undertaken, the interviewers were of the opinion that training uptake was supply-led in that, for the most part, it depended on what was on offer from the trade association. Training uptake also appeared to be price sensitive, particularly for credit unions in Groups Two and Three. In addition, the programme timetable (for example, evenings or all day) and the place of delivery (in-house or outside location) all appeared to influence uptake by credit unions. The tenor of the following comment by Credit Union O was echoed by a number of the credit unions interviewed:

> "ABCUL do courses that are fully manualed and everything else, but you pay big time for them. They're full day courses as well, so there's no doubt that the quality of the course is first class, but the way in which it's delivered doesn't suit our needs. CEIS (Community Enterprise in Scotland) were prepared to deliver the training in a way which suited our needs. For example, if one module normally takes a day to deliver, CEIS split it over three evenings. They came here from 5 until 8 for three Monday evenings."

Appropriate training is important in the development of a successful board. Leighton and Thain (1997) highlight the importance of 'introducing new directors to the job' without which the contribution made by the director is deferred and their comfort level is lessened. In a similar vein, Multiculturalism and Citizenship Canada (1992) cited 'limited training and orientation' as a detriment and impediment to the development of successful boards.

Final thoughts on performance differences

Isolating factors pivotal in driving performance differences between credit unions is not without problems as different business models are utilised by credit unions. In the UK, discussion about business models tends to centre on the relative virtues of the new model versus the ethical/traditional model. However, this analysis suggests that this debate may be more about theoretical mindsets than hard realities, primarily because, for a credit union to be effective, irrespective of its label, it must satisfy conditions such as serving the financial needs of a varied membership base, offer a good return on members' funds, provide appropriate products, operate efficiently, demonstrate financial discipline and be subject to appropriate governance structures.

In our discussions with the better performing Group One credit unions, the importance they attached to having good quality, centrally located premises was apparent. This is not to say that a poorly performing credit union can be transformed through refurbishing existing or acquiring new premises. Rather, there appears to be an appropriate point in a credit union's growth cycle when such activities will give a further pronounced impetus to membership and asset growth.

Credit unions with appropriately skilled and motivated manager/management teams, and appropriately skilled and motivated boards of directors, significantly outperformed counterparty credit unions. Our analysis suggested that in many cases it was the board of directors which was not functioning to its full capacity, with this more of a problem for smaller credit unions which did not have the necessary resources to appoint paid employees. Also evident was that many credit unions did not meet the WOCCU (2002) 'job prerequisites'. Areas of failure for both weak and strong credit unions were 'knowledge of risk management and effective management', 'familiarity with asset liability management' and 'familiarity with marketing concepts'. However, more worryingly, many boards have a considerable number of directors with no 'ability to read and interpret financial statements'.

Creating better functioning boards is not a simple task because many of the credit unions studied faced member apathy manifesting itself in difficulty in attracting members to serve on the board. Within this context, it was also the case that the training of directors can go a significant way to improving the performance of the board and ultimately the credit union. Training can range from potential directors shadowing existing directors to buying in training to meet the specific needs of the credit union. It was noted that for Group Two and Group Three credit unions, training was both price sensitive and time sensitive with credit unions arguing that training was too expensive and not usually available at times best suited to a volunteer board.

Summary and policy recommendations

The overview of the financial measures and Data Envelopment Analysis (DEA) efficiency scores highlighted that there is weakness in the UK credit union movement. A question mark was raised over the long-term survival of at least 50% of credit unions in Great Britain (GB). While structural weakness also exists for certain credit unions in Northern Ireland (NI), the number is relatively small.

There are clear differences in the business models used by credit unions. In the study, the ethical/ traditional model of credit union development which underpins nearly all credit unions in NI has been juxtaposed in GB with a new model of credit union development centred on seven doctrines of success. This new model has become interwoven with efforts to fast track the growth of credit unions through the provision of grants used by credit unions to appoint employees and acquire premises. The debate between the traditional and modern models may, however, be more about theoretical mindsets than hard realities, primarily because, for a credit union to be effective, irrespective of its label, it must satisfy conditions such as serving the financial needs of a varied membership base, offer a good return on members' funds, provide appropriate products, operate efficiently, demonstrate financial discipline and be subject to appropriate governance structures.

The success of credit unions in NI is in part due to their being organisations inspired by the community for the community, and also recognising from the outset that their long-term viability requires that they attract a cross section of people from local communities, and not just those who are socially or financially excluded. The discussion stressed that the needs of the socially and financially excluded are best served not by credit unions concentrating exclusively on low-income communities – that simply circulates money among the poor and creates financial exclusion ghettos – but by mobilising the monies of the rich as well as the poor. In GB, certain credit unions have fallen into the trap of over-focusing on low-income communities, thus creating the perception of credit unions as the poor man's bank and, in so doing, hindering the development of these credit unions, and, indeed, the movement as a whole in GB.

In recognition that a certain scale of operation is required for credit unions to function effectively, many credit unions in GB have sought to extend their common bond, the trend being for occupational and residential common bonds to be extended to 'live or work'. In so doing, there is an explicit recognition that to be successful credit unions must have scope to diversify their membership mix. Accepting this point, it must also be emphasised that too wide a common bond may negate its purpose, which is to increase the likelihood that members will know each other and, in turn, have a sense of loyalty and commitment to a joint enterprise and thus, through moral suasion, minimise loan default. As credit unions extend their common bond, they must therefore increasingly utilise credit-scoring mechanisms prior to the provision of loans to members.

Since 2001, credit union amalgamations have gathered pace in GB. No simple explanation can be offered regarding the motivation and consequences of these mergers. It was, however, noted that the merger, particularly when due to a transfer of engagements from weak or failing credit unions, has tended to have negative consequences for the healthier party, such as diluting its focus on its own members, increasing the level of arrears and reducing dividend payments. In many cases, the cooperative spirit has been paramount in driving through such mergers, particularly when failure would have led to the loss of funds by members. The advent, since 2002, of the Financial Services Compensation Scheme may, however, encourage stronger credit unions to increasingly shy away from merging with weaker entities, with failure the better option for all parties concerned.

Another trend in GB post 2001 has been the formation of new 'fast growth' credit unions. In general, these credit unions have received significant levels of support from their local authorities, which has enabled them, from the outset, to have in place high-specification premises and a team of paid employees. This hothouse approach to credit union establishment contrasts with the more traditional/ethical volunteer-focused and evolutionary nature of credit union establishment and development. These new credit unions are concerned, and rightly so, with providing a service to those who might otherwise face financial exclusion, with aspects of their funding dependent on providing this service. However, in the long term, success for these credit unions is dependent on attracting a cross section of members from their local communities.

Sustainability is an issue for merging, 'fast growth' and credit unions generally. Failure to achieve sustainability runs the risk of creating a dependency culture. Credit unions are founded on the principle of self-help and outside funding weakens and dilutes this principle. Outside funding may also encourage a credit union to take decisions which might not be undertaken under normal growth conditions and which, in the longer term, may be detrimental to the stable development of the credit union. At some stage, the ability of certain credit unions to access grants and subsidies may well come to an end. Replacing a supportive environment with one of no support is, however, unacceptable. An alternative, which would not damage the principle of self-help nor hamper normal growth, is that grants should only be accessed when credit unions were undertaking work in, say, the area of financial inclusion, and had predicted that the ensuing revenue streams were unlikely to cover overhead costs.

Our analysis also highlighted that credit unions with an appropriately skilled and motivated manager/management team, and an appropriately skilled and motivated board of directors, significantly outperformed counterparty credit unions. It was evident from the case investigations that many credit unions did not meet the World Council of Credit Unions (WOCCU) (2002) 'job prerequisites'. Areas of failure for both weak and strong credit unions were 'knowledge of risk management and effective management', 'familiarity with asset liability management' and 'familiarity with marketing concepts'. However, more worryingly, many boards have a considerable number of directors with no 'ability to read and interpret financial statements'.

The creation of better functioning boards is not a simple task. In the first instance, member apathy is a problem. A recurring theme was the difficulty that credit unions face in attracting members to serve on the credit union board, although it was noted that a very small number operated a nominating committee. Noting these constraints, training of directors can go a significant way in improving the performance of the board and, ultimately, the credit union. Training can range from potential directors shadowing existing directors to buying in training to meet the specific needs of the credit union. Training uptake was supply-led in that it depended on what was made available, primarily by the trade association. It was also noted that, for smaller credit unions, training was both price and time sensitive. Government financial support, channelled through the trade associations, could be profitably utilised both to extend the range of training on offer and to subsidise its cost to the credit union.

No benchmark data is readily available to enable individual credit unions to assess how well they are performing and how performance might be improved. DEA and PEARLS were described as two techniques capable of achieving an assessment framework of credit unions. Given the stage of development of UK credit unions, PEARLS is likely to be the more acceptable benchmark mechanism. The efficacy of PEARLS for UK credit unions would be best served by focusing on a subset of key PEARLS, and by providing each credit union with these key PEARLS plus appropriate benchmark measures dictated by credit union size bands and common bond type. This benchmark data could, for example, refer to average values for the top quartile of credit union performers for each of PEARLS measures, and would be provided to credit unions on a quarterly basis.

One byproduct of the changes in Credit Union regulation in recent years is that although credit union financial returns made to the previous regulator – the Registrar of Friendly Societies – were considered to be in the public domain, legislative change has transformed the status of this data, as the data are now considered to be confidential. The Financial Services Authority (FSA), the current regulator of credit union affairs, is prohibited by the 2000 Financial Services and Markets Act from placing this material in the public domain. The effect of this confidentiality requirement serves as a real barrier to independent scrutiny of the sector by researchers, and implications of the legislative change referred to earlier are regrettable.

Our analysis has been based on hard empirical evidence about the relative performance of UK credit unions, and our recommendations now outlined are drawn directly from this evidence. We base the recommendations that follow on our assumptions about what constitutes an effective credit union – namely, that a credit union should serve the financial needs of a varied membership base, offer a good return on members' funds, provide appropriate products, operate efficiently, demonstrate financial discipline and be subject to appropriate governance structures. These assumptions about an effective credit union hold good regardless of whether they are traditional/ethical credit unions or modern 'fast growth' credit unions. Our recommendations have the dual aim of rectifying weaknesses we have identified through our studies and offering a platform to build on the achievements of stronger performing credit unions. We believe that, only by learning what lessons we can from better performing credit unions, will the UK credit union movement better serve disadvantaged communities.

Our key recommendations are meant to be constructive, and hopefully they can assist the credit union movement in the ongoing debate about the development of strong, sustainable, self-help credit unions that can positively contribute to the financial well-being of their members. The recommendations are variously directed at individual credit unions [C], government [G] and the trade bodies [T]. After each recommendation, the stakeholder(s) to which the recommendation is addressed is highlighted.

Policy recommendations

1. Credit union development that concentrates solely on serving the needs of the financially excluded is inherently weak. Development based on a cross section of the population, including affluent sections of society, offers a more viable long-term model. Greater emphasis should be given to this by credit unions, trade associations and the government. [C, G, T]

2. The current trend towards widening of common bonds should be actively encouraged, especially where this facilitates a diversification of membership mix by credit unions. [C, G, T]

3.   The widening of common bonds should be accompanied by greater use of credit scoring for loan purposes, given that direct knowledge of members will be diluted and bad debt might otherwise increase without credit scoring. [C, T]

4.   It is not in the interests of the credit union movement to expect strong credit unions to merge with weaker ones if the result is a weakening in the position of the former. [C, G, T]

5.   Given the critical role of volunteer credit union boards, more investment must be made in the training and development of the volunteers who serve on them. [C, G, T]

6.   The role of volunteers and their use by credit unions should be further investigated in a dedicated study that takes account of the changing demand for volunteers as affected, for instance, by the growth of professionalism in credit unions, and also the supply of volunteers and the continuing evolution of volunteering policy and practice in different parts of the UK. [G, T]

7.   Relying on grants to fund the core business of credit unions leads to a dependency culture that ultimately is not conducive to sustainable development. Subvention provided to credit unions should be 'targeted' to particular areas of need (for example, financial exclusion) but not used to fund core business activities or as a substitute for self-reliance on sufficient revenue generated by credit unions themselves. [C, G,]

8.   Greater attention needs to be given to the potential for 'shared services provision' by UK credit unions, particularly in relation to IT. A scoping study supported by all the trade associations would be beneficial. [G, T]

9.   The benchmarking of credit union performance through a selected subset of metrics from the PEARLS system should be implemented by either government or the trade associations for all credit unions, and associated training should be provided. [G, T]

10.   Good research requires access to timely and detailed data at the level of the individual entity. Credit union financial data submitted under the regulatory regime of the FSA are, because of legislative change introduced by the 2000 Financial Services and Markets Act, legally confidential. This barrier to independent scrutiny of the sector by not having access to individual credit union data (which was previously in the public domain) is regrettable and needs to be rectified by legislative change. [G]

References

ABCUL (Association of British Credit Unions) (2004) An introduction to PEARLS in Britain (www.abcul.org/lib/liDownload/44/PEARLS%20in%20the%20UK.pdf)

Berthoud, R. and Hinton, T. (1989) *Credit unions in the United Kingdom*, Policy Studies Institute, Research Report 693.

Black, H. and Dugger, R. (1981) 'Credit union structure, growth and regulatory problems', *Journal of Finance*, vol XXXVI, no 2, pp 529-38.

Branch B. and Baker C. (1998) 'Credit union governance: unique challenges', *Nexus*, no 41, pp 1-6.

Brown, R., O'Connor, I. and Brown, R. (1997) 'Measurement of efficiency in not-for-profit financial intermediaries: Australasian evidence', The 10th Annual Australasian Finance and Banking Conference, The University of New South Wales.

Burger, A. (1993) Foreword to H.O. Fried and C.A.K. Lovell *Evaluating the performance of credit unions*, Madison, WI: Filene Research Institute and The Center for Credit Union Research.

Centre for Economic Development and Area Regeneration (2000) *Credit union development activity in Scotland*, Edinburgh: Scottish Executive.

Chapman, M., Boyle, A., Rutherford, F. and Wagner, F. (2004) *Credit union training and skills audit*, Edinburgh: Scottish Executive.

Chmura Economics and Analytics (2004) *An assessment of the competitive environment between credit unions and banks*, Springfield: VA:The Thomas Jefferson Institute for Public Policy, May.

Clutton-Brock, O. (1996) *Credit unions in Great Britain: A review of the years 1979-1995*, London: Registry of Friendly Societies, pp 1-21.

Collins, G. (2003) 'The economic case for mergers: old, new, borrowed, and blue', *Journal of Economic Issues*, December, vol 37, no 4, p. 987.

Combined Code (2003) *The Combined Code on corporate governance*, London: Financial Reporting Council.

Committee on the Financial Aspects of Corporate Governance (1992) *Report with Code of Best Practice* (Cadbury Report), London: Gee Publishing.

DETI (NI) (Department of Enterprise, Trade and Investment, Northern Ireland) (2004) *Credit unions and Industrial Provident Societies review, initial consultation for proposals for modernisation of Northern Ireland policy on credit unions and Industrial and Provident Societies*, Belfast: DETI (NI).

Donnelly, R.D. (2002) 'British credit unions at the crossroads', International Cooperative Alliance Conference, Greece, 9-12 May.

Donnelly, R.D. and Kahn, H. (1999) *A report into the rapid growth of credit unions in Scotland*, Edinburgh: Royal Bank of Scotland plc and Heriot-Watt University.

Fairbairn, B., Ketilson, L. and Krebs, P. (1997) *Credit unions and community economic development*, Centre for the Study of Cooperatives, University of Saskatchewan, Canada.

Fried, H.O. and Lovell, C.A.K. (1993) Evaluating the performance of credit unions, Madison, WI: Filene Research Institute and The Center for Credit Union Research.

Fried, H.O., Lovell, C.A.K. and Yaisawarng, S. (1999) 'The impact of mergers on credit union service provision', *Journal of Banking and Finance*, vol 23, pp 237-386.

FSA (Financial Services Authority) (2001a) *The credit unions sourcebook*, London: HM Treasury.

FSA (2001b) *Mutual societies annual statistics* (www.fsa.gov.uk/pubs/annual/report_mutuals.pdf).

FSA (2002) 'New milestone for FSA credit union regulation', FSA press release (www.fsa.gov.uk/pages/library/communication/PR/2002/002.shtml)

FSA (2004) *Credit unions annual statistics* (www.fsa.gov.uk/Pages/Doing/small_firms/unions/pdf/stats04.pdf)

Fuller D. (1998) 'Credit union development: financial inclusion and exclusion', *Geoforum*, vol 29, no 2, pp 145-57.

Griffiths, G. and Howells, G. (1991) 'Slumbering giant or white elephant: do credit unions have a role to play in the UK credit market?', *NILQ*, vol 42, pp 199-211.

Hayton, K. (2001) 'The role of Scottish credit unions in tackling financial exclusion', *Policy & Politics*, vol 29, no 3, pp 291-7.

Hayton, K., Gray, L. and Stirling, K. (2005) *Scottish credit unions: Meeting member demands and needs*, Edinburgh: Scottish Executive.

Heenan, D. and McLaughlin, R. (2002) 'Re-assessing the role of credit unions in community development: a case study of Derry Credit Union, Northern Ireland', *Community Development Journal*, vol 37, no 3, July, pp 249-59.

HM Treasury (1999) *Credit unions of the future*, Taskforce report, November, London: HM Stationery Office.

HM Treasury (2004) *Promoting financial inclusion*, December, London: HM Stationery Office.

HM Treasury (2005) *The credit union interest rate cap*, March, London: HM Stationery Office.

Jones, P.A. (1999) *Towards sustainable credit union development*, Research report, ABCUL.

Jones, P.A. (2001) *From small acorns to strong oaks: A study into the development of credit unions in rural England*, Research report, Countryside Agency.

Jones, P.A. (2003) *Growing credit unions in the West Midlands: The case for restructuring* (www.abcul.org/lib/lidownload/56/growing_credit_unions_paul_jones_0304.pdf).

Jones, P.A. (2004) *Creating wealth in the West Midlands through sustainable credit unions: Interim report*, March (www.abcul.org/lib/lidownload/55/interim%20report%20paul%20jones%20march202004.pdf).

Leighton, D. and Thain, D. (1997) *Making boards work: What directors must do to make Canadian boards effective*, Toronto: McGraw Hill Hyerson.

McKillop, D.G. and Wilson, J. (2003) 'Credit unions in Britain: A time for change', *Public Money and Management*, vol 23, pp 119-23.

McKillop, D.G., Glass J.C. and Ferguson, C. (2002) 'Investigating the cost performance of UK credit unions using radial and non-radial efficiency measures', *Journal of Banking & Finance*, vol 26, p 8, pp 1563-91.

Multiculturalism and Citizenship Canada (1992) *Why people volunteer*, Report to the Voluntary Action Directorate Multiculturalism and Citizenship Canada, Ontario: Canada.

North, D.C. (2000) 'A revolution in economics', in C. Menard (ed) *Institutions, contracts and organisation*, Cheltenham: Edward Elgar, pp 37-41.

Pille, P. and Paradi, J.C. (2002) 'Financial performance analysis of Ontario (Canada), Credit unions: an application of DEA in the regulatory environment', *European Journal of Operational Research*, vol 139, no 2, pp 339-50.

Ralston, D., Wright, A. and Garden, K. (2001) 'Can mergers ensure the survival of credit unions in the third millennium?', *Journal of Banking and Finance*, vol 25, pp 2277-304.

Reifner, U. (1997) 'New financial products for inclusive banking', in J. Rossiter, *Financial exclusion: Can mutuality fill the gap?*, London: New Policy Institute and the UK Social Investment Forum, pp 16-21.

Rhoades, S.A. (1998) 'The efficiency effects of bank mergers: an overview of case studies of nine mergers', *Journal of Banking and Finance*, vol 22, pp 273-91.

Richardson, D.C. (2002) *PEARLS monitoring system*, World Council of Credit Unions Toolkit Series, no. 4 (www.woccu.org).

Roe, M.J. (1993) 'Takeover politics', in M.M. Blair (ed.) *The deal decade*, Washington DC: The Brookings Institute, pp 321-52.

Ryder, N. (2001) 'Friend or foe? The FSA and credit unions', *Business Law Review*, July, pp 169-73.

Ryder, N. (2002) 'Credit unions and financial exclusion: the odd couple?', *Journal of Social Welfare and Family Law*, vol 24, no 4, pp 423-34.

Sibbald, A., Ferguson, C. and McKillop, D. (2002) 'An examination of key factors of influence in the development process of credit union industries', *Annals of Public and Cooperative Economics*, vol 73, no 2, pp 399-428.

Strachan, D. (2001) *Financial Services Authority press release*, FSA/PN/107/2001, 23 August, London: Financial Services Authority.

Walne, T. (2002) 'Clampdown shakes up the credit unions', *Financial Mail on Sunday*, September 22.

Ward, A-M. and McKillop, D. (2005a) 'The law of proportionate effect: the growth of the UK credit union movement at national and regional level', *Journal of Business, Finance and Accounting*, vol 32, no 9 and 10, pp 1827-59.

Ward, A-M. and McKillop, D. (2005b) 'An investigation into the link between UK credit union characteristics, location and their success', *Annals of Public and Cooperative Economics*, vol 76, no 3, pp 461-90.

Welsh Assembly Government (2004) *Social Justice Report*, March (www.wales.gov.uk/themessocialdeprivation/content/soc-just-report-2004-e.pdf).

WOCCU (World Council of Credit Unions) Inc. (2002) *Development of best practices in credit union supervision*, December 4, Madison, WI: WOCCU.

WOCCU Inc. (2003) *Statistical report, financials and annual report*, Madison, WI: WOCCU.

Worthington, A.C. (1998 [96 on p) 'The determinants of non-bank financial institution efficiency: a stochastic cost frontier approach', *Applied Financial Economics*, vol 8, pp 287-97.

Appendix

Table A1: Summary data by size category (England and Wales, Scotland), 2001

England and Wales	A>£2m	£1m<A<£2m	£0.5m<A <£1m	A<£0.5m	Total
Number	14	15	26	464	519
% of total	2.7%	2.9%	5.0%	89.4%	100.0%
Assets (£)	63,600,503	20,713,464	18,223,656	42,934,461	145,472,084
% of total	43.7%	14.2%	12.5%	29.5%	100.0%
Members	53,554	24,970	21,638	118,601	218,763
% of total	24.5%	11.4%	9.9%	54.2%	100.0%
Shares, savings/ member (£)	955	745	743	305	557
Scotland	A>£2m	£1m<A<£2m	£0.5m<A<£1m	A<£0.5m	Total
Number	8	10	9	107	134
% of total	6.0%	7.5%	6.7%	79.9%	100.0%
Assets (£)	80,288,114	14,161,498	6,625,192	16,543,947	117,618,751
% of total	68.3%	12.0%	5.6%	14.1%	100.0%
Members	64,400	21,782	11,196	45,117	142,495
% of total	45.2%	15.3%	7.9%	31.7%	100.0%
Shares, savings/ member (£)	1,024	571	513	308	688

Table A2: Selection of performance measures (England and Wales, Scotland), 2001

England and Wales	Group 1	Group 2	Group 3	Group 4	Overall
Members	930	374	229	151	422
Member change	16.4%	18.9%	12.3%	6.6%	15.4%
Shares/member (£)	757	384	259	204	557
Loans/shares	94.2%	81.4%	63.2%	54.5%	89.1%
Operating expenditure/ operating income	46.4%	100.6%	153.1%	218.1%	62.5%
Loan provisions/average loans	2.0%	10.2%	16.2%	23.3%	4.2%
Net interest received/average loans	10.7%	10.8%	10.6%	12.2%	10.8%
Return/average members' funds	5.4%	2.6%	2.0%	0.9%	4.6%
Capital/assets	8.2%	6.0%	5.5%	1.1%	7.5%
Scotland	**Group 1**	**Group 2**	**Group 3**	**Group 4**	**Overall**
Members	2788	737	467	219	1063
Member change	10.6%	13.9%	11.4%	−23.3%	8.8%
Shares/member (£)	845	405	320	396	688
Loans/shares	102.7%	99.9%	84.7%	69.3%	100.6%
Operating expenditure/ operating income	31.9%	66.1%	77.9%	128.6%	39.3%
Delinquent loans/average loans	2.1%	9.9%	16.0%	14.2%	3.7%
Loan provisions/average loans	1.2%	3.5%	4.9%	4.4%	1.7%
Net interest received/average loans	11.2%	11.1%	10.9%	11.5%	11.1%
Return/average members' funds	6.9%	3.1%	2.4%	1.6%	6.1%
Capital/assets	12.1%	8.6%	7.9%	5.7%	11.4%

Table A3: Data envelopment analysis (DEA), (England and Wales, Scotland), 2001

England and Wales DEA	Group 1	Group 2	Group 3	Group 4	Overall
Efficiency score	0.5573	0.3609	0.2888	0.2240	0.3580
Efficient CUs (number of)	18	8	1	1	28
CUs with peers	17	8	0	1	26
Total peer count	735	865	0	50	1650
DRS (Number subject to)	125	119	116	97	457
IRS (Number subject to)	2	6	12	30	50
Scotland DEA	**Group 1**	**Group 2**	**Group 3**	**Group 4**	**Overall**
Efficiency score	0.6193	0.4546	0.4393	0.4464	0.4906
Efficient CUs (number of)	7	1	3	6	17
CUs with peers	6	1	2	2	11
Total peer count	242	86	48	13	389
DRS (Number subject to)	15	9	1	3	28
IRS (Number subject to)	13	20	27	29	89